Looking Forward with Hope

Looking Forward With Hope

Reflections on the Present State and Future of Theological Education

EDITED BY
Benjamín Valentín

CASCADE *Books* • Eugene, Oregon

LOOKING FORWARD WITH HOPE
Reflections on the Present State and Future of Theological Education

Copyright © 2019 Wipf and Stock Publishers. All rights reserved. Except for brief quotations in critical publications or reviews, no part of this book may be reproduced in any manner without prior written permission from the publisher. Write: Permissions, Wipf and Stock Publishers, 199 W. 8th Ave., Suite 3, Eugene, OR 97401.

Cascade Books
An Imprint of Wipf and Stock Publishers
199 W. 8th Ave., Suite 3
Eugene, OR 97401

www.wipfandstock.com

PAPERBACK ISBN: 978-1-4982-3013-1
HARDCOVER ISBN: 978-1-4982-3015-5
EBOOK ISBN: 978-1-4982-3014-8

Cataloguing-in-Publication data:

Names: Benjamin Valentin, editor.
Title: Looking forward with hope : reflections on the present state and future of theological education / edited by Benjamin Valentin.
Description: Eugene, OR: Cascade Books, p. ; cm. —Includes bibliographical references.
Identifiers: ISBN 978-1-4982-3013-1 (paperback) | ISBN 978-1-4982-3015-5 (hardcover) | ISBN 978-1-4982-3014-8 (ebook)
Subjects: 1. Theological seminaries—United States. 2. Theology—Study and teaching—United States.
Classification: BV4030 .L54 2019 (print) | CALL NUMBER (ebook)

Manufactured in the U.S.A.

Contents

Contributors vii

Introduction xi
    BENJAMÍN VALENTÍN

1. First But Not Finished:
Mainline Protestant Theological Education 1
    DANIEL O. ALESHIRE

2. America's Changing Religious and Cultural Landscape
and Its Implications for Theological Education 34
    NANCY T. AMMERMAN

3. Embracing a Greater, Higher Calling: Redefining the Mission
and Purpose of the Freestanding Protestant Seminary 43
    BENJAMÍN VALENTÍN

4. A House Built on Sand?
A Blunt Look at the Assumptions of Theological Education 68
    NICK CARTER

5. From Resistance to Resurrection: Meadville Lombard's
TouchPoint Model of Theological Education 90
    SHARON D. WELCH AND MICHAEL S. HOGUE

Contents

6. A Reform Amounting to a Revolution: New York Theological Seminary and Theological Education for the City 104
   DALE T. IRVIN

7. The Change We Need:
Race and Ethnicity in Theological Education 129
   WILLIE JAMES JENNINGS

8. Why Seminaries and the Churches Should Welcome Religious Diversity in the USA 138
   HEIDI HADSELL

Contributors

Daniel O. Aleshire served as executive director of The Association of Theological Schools in the United States and Canada (ATS) for nineteen years until he retired from that post in June 30, 2017. A frequent speaker worldwide, Dr. Aleshire has written extensively on issues of ministry and theological education. His works include *Earthen Vessels: Hopeful Reflections on the Work and Future of Theological Schools* (Eerdmans, 2008). Dr. Aleshire taught at The Southern Baptist Theological Seminary from 1978 to 1990.

Nancy T. Ammerman is Professor of Sociology of Religion in the Sociology Department of the College of Arts and Sciences and in the School of Theology at Boston University. She also serves as Associate Dean of the Faculty for the Social Sciences in the college. Dr. Ammerman's influential works include *Sacred Stories, Spiritual Tribes: Finding Religion in Everyday Life* (Oxford University Press, 2013) and the well-known *Bible Believers: Fundamentalists in the Modern World* (Rutgers University Press, 1987). Her most recent research has focused on the social structures and practices of everyday lived religion. Earlier in her career, she spent many years studying congregations.

Nick Carter is currently serving as Interim President at the American Baptist Seminary of the West in Berkeley, California. In 2014 he retired after ten years as President of Andover Newton Theological School in Newton Centre, Massachusetts. He previously pastored a large church in Massachusetts and served on the

Contributors

ABCUSA denominational staff in New York City. Dr. Carter was also the National Executive Director of SANE/FREEZE, a grassroots nuclear arms control group, and the Vice President of a for-profit marketing communications company.

Heidi Hadsell is President and Professor of Social Ethics at Hartford Seminary in Hartford, Connecticut. Previously she served as Director of the World Council of Churches' Ecumenical Institute in Bossey, Switzerland. She also served as Dean of McCormick Theological Seminary in Chicago. Dr. Hadsell has a deep commitment to interfaith dialogue and engagement, and is widely published in the areas of ecumenism, environmental ethics, interreligious relations, and the public role of religion in society. She is co-editor of *Overcoming Fundamentalism: Ethical Responses from Five Continents* (Globethics, 2009).

Michael Hogue is Professor of Theology at Meadville Lombard Theological School in Chicago. His teaching and writing explores theology as it intersects with environmental ethics, American culture and politics, globalization, and the sciences. Dr. Hogue's articles and reviews have appeared in many journals. He is also the author of two monographs, *The Promise of Religious Naturalism* (Rowman and Littlefield, 2010) and *The Tangled Bank: Toward an Ecotheological Ethics of Responsible Participation* (Pickwick, 2008). He is at work on a third monograph that aims to develop an American religious naturalist political theology.

Dale T. Irvin is President and Professor of World Christianity at New York Theological Seminary in New York City. His teaching and research interests focus on the history of the Christian movement and global Christianity. With Scott W. Sunquist, he co-authored *History of the World Christian Movement*, a two-volume work published by Orbis Books. He is also editor of *The Protestant Reformation and World Christianity: Global Perspectives* (Eerdmans, 2017). Dr. Irvin is a founding editor of *The Journal of World Christianity* and serves on the editorial board of *The Living Pulpit*.

CONTRIBUTORS

He is an ordained minister in the American Baptist Churches USA and is a member of The Riverside Church in New York City.

Willie James Jennings is Associate Professor of Systematic Theology and Africana Studies at Yale University Divinity School. Before joining the Yale faculty, he taught at Duke Divinity School where he also served as Dean of the Faculty for many years. Dr. Jennings' book *The Christian Imagination: Theology and the Origins of Race* (Yale University Press, 2010) won the American Academy of Religion Award of Excellence in the Study of Religion in the Constructive-Reflective category and also won the Grawemeyer Award in Religion. His most recent work is a theological commentary on the biblical book of Acts. Writing in the areas of liberation theology, cultural identities, and theological anthropology, he has authored more than forty scholarly essays and nearly two dozen reviews. Jennings is an ordained Baptist minister and has served as interim pastor for several North Carolina churches.

Benjamín Valentín is Associate Professor of Latinx Christianity at Yale University Divinity School. A native of New York City and born of Puerto Rican parents, Dr. Valentin taught at Andover Newton Theological School in Newton Centre, Massachusetts, where he was Professor of Theology and Culture and Director of the Orlando E. Costas Lectureship in Latino/a Religion and Theology before joining the Yale faculty in 2016. His teaching and research interests are in contemporary theology and culture; US Latino/a Christianity and theology; Christianity in Latin America; liberation theology; and constructive theology. He is the author of the award-winning *Mapping Public Theology: Beyond Culture, Identity, and Difference* (winner of the Hispanic Theological Initiative's 2003 Latino/a Book of the Year Award: Bloomsbury T&T Clark, 2002) and *Theological Cartographies: Mapping the Encounter with God, Humanity, and Christ* (Westminster John Knox Press, 2015). Dr. Valentin is also editor of four other published edited volumes, and is seen nationally and internationally as a premier interpreter of US Latino/a theology and liberation theology.

Contributors

Sharon D. Welch is Professor of Religion and Society at Meadville Lombard Theological School in Chicago. She served as Provost at Meadville Lombard Theological School from 2007 to 2017. Dr. Welch is the author of numerous articles and five books, including the widely influential *A Feminist Ethic of Risk* (Fortress, 1989) and *After Empire: The Art and Ethos of Enduring Peace* (Fortress, 2004). Her published works explore the intersections of religion, social ethics, women's and gender studies, globalization, and educational leadership. Dr. Welch is a Senior Fellow of the Institute for Humanist Studies, a member of the International Steering Committee of Global Action to Prevent War, and a member of the Unitarian Universalist Peace Ministry Network. Before joining Meadville Lombard Theological School, she was a Professor and Chair of Religious Studies at the University of Missouri-Columbia. Dr. Welch began her career at Harvard Divinity School, where she served as Assistant and then Associate Professor of Theology and Religion and Society from 1982 to 1991.

Introduction

Benjamín Valentín

ADMINISTRATORS, TRUSTEES, BOARD MEMBERS, and faculty members at theological schools say that they are in a state of crisis. This sense of crisis is fostering much discussion about the future of such schools and the future of theological education more generally. The fretful conversations are understandable. The truth is that theological schools are facing a perfect storm of jeopardies that threatens their future prospects and even their survival. The storm is all the more menacing for free-standing or independent seminaries that are not connected to a university, and especially for free-standing/independent mainline Protestant seminaries. Used to dealing with the vulnerability that comes with their smaller scale and unallied status, now they are encountering other challenges as well. The growing disinterest in organized religion and the softening involvement in traditional religion in American society; the decline of liberal or mainline Protestant churches and denominations; the declining attractiveness of ecclesiastical leadership as a career choice among young people and especially among men; the marginalization or devaluation of theological studies in certain sectors of the academy and in the churches and general society; the marked and precipitous drop in student enrollment; the disadvantageous circumstances generated by the recent economic downturn in the United States; the fall-off in financial contributions from friends, denominations, foundations, and other traditional supporters of the enterprise of theological education; the wearing effect of bad organization, inadequate management, and insufficient preparedness to raise funds in a changing religious climate: these are more recent developments that pose a challenge to theological schools, and especially to free-standing mainline Protestant or mainline denominational theological schools.[1]

Those who are affiliated with and work within these schools see this perfect storm of jeopardies as threatening to compromise the future of theological schools and theological education more generally. For discussions at these schools are about the state of theological education and theological schools; about the changes that need to take place in theological education and in theological schools; and about the new visions, strategies, initiatives, educational models, forms of governance, mergers, investments, and capital ventures that need to be embraced and undertaken if free-standing/independent theological schools are to survive and thrive.

These discussions are often tinged with a sense of urgency. Yet they also manifest a strong consensus that mainline Protestant and mainline denominational seminaries do important work and serve an important purpose. Besides helping to prepare leaders for religious vocation in many different settings, they contribute to intellectual life by grooming academics, teachers, writers, analysts, and researchers of all kinds. They also foster greater religious literacy in our society, which is no small thing in our times. And they seek to abet sensibilities, dispositions, virtues, and values that can make the good citizen. In these and in other ways, such theological schools contribute to the life of the church, the academy, and society as a whole. And yet denominational seminaries recognize that the whole enterprise of theological education is in a state of crisis and in need of general examination and repair due

---

1. For more on some of these social, religious, and ecclesiastical trends in the United States, see Chaves, *American Religion*. Some of the essays in this volume explore these trends further.

INTRODUCTION

to the new realities and challenges mentioned above. This is fueling much discussion of the many challenges mainline Protestant and/or mainline denominational seminaries face today, and much discussion of the kind of changes that need to occur within them and in theological education in general.

This book contributes to this ongoing discussion of the present state and possible future of mainline Protestant and mainline denominational theological education more generally and of free-standing mainline Protestant and denominational theological schools in the United States especially.[2] It does so by bringing together a diverse cast of administrators and professors working within different theological schools to reflect on this complicated question from their various perspectives and institutional settings and experiences. Discussions of theological education and theological schooling abound, but rarely does one find these conveyed in a book. Rarer still is a book that offers various perspectives on the question of the present state and future of mainline Protestant or mainline denominational theological schools and theological education. The few books on the market that address this multifaceted question are single-author monographs.[3] Some of these are also a little bit dated, reflecting, therefore, the challenges, concerns, questions, and assumptions of another era even

---

2. This book will not focus on the situation of theological schools that are either affiliated with or linked to the Evangelical Churches or the Roman Catholic Churches. It will focus on the status of theological schools that have been historically or predominantly associated with or linked to denominations and churches that are often referred to as the "mainline denominations and churches." This designation typically includes the following church bodies: The United Methodist Church; the Evangelical Lutheran Church in America (ELCA); the Presbyterian Church (USA); the Episcopal Church; the American Baptist Churches in the USA; the United Church of Christ (UCC); and the Christian Church (Disciples of Christ). The term can sometimes also include churches or congregations belonging to the Unitarian Universalist Association (UUA). On the matter of contextual focus, I will note that this book also focuses on the context of theological education and schooling in the United States of America.

3. For example, see Aleshire, *Earthen Vessels*, and Gonzalez, *The History of Theological Education*.

XIII

if only from just a few decades ago.[4] But much has changed with respect to the context of theological education in the last two or three decades. And so, while possibly still pertinent, the concerns and interests of some of these books may no longer be paramount. Various edited volumes on the topic of theological education focus almost exclusively on matters of pedagogy and do not address concerns regarding the present predicament and future viability of theological schooling more generally.[5] This volume addresses these concerns from a wider perspective, tendering essays written by different authors with different experiences, vocational roles, institutional settings, and points of view.

Because the crisis in theological education seems to have affected free-standing or independent mainline Protestant and mainline denominational theological schools in the United States especially, most of the following essays focus on the challenges and the prospects of such schools. Most of their authors come from these kinds of schools. But a few of the essays in the volume describe university-based theological schools, and they address concerns that apply to the industry and the vocation of theological education more generally. Together, these essays address a broad range of issues that mainline Protestant or ecumenical theological education faces and prospective paths of reappraisal and recreation that are either being pursued by some theological schools or that can be considered by theological schools more generally.

The book's first essay—"First But Not Finished: Mainline Protestant Theological Education"—starts us off in a very appropriate and useful way. Essentially, it provides a bird's-eye, panoramic view of the current situation of mainline Protestant theological schools by placing it in the light of the wider context of the history of mainline Protestant theological education. Written by Daniel Aleshire, former executive director of the Association

---

4. For example, see Farley, *Theologia*; Kelsey, *To Understand God Truly* and *Between Athens and Berlin*; and Messer, *Calling Church & Seminary into the 21st Century*.

5. See, for instance, Jones and Paulsell, eds., *The Scope of Our Art*, and Barker and Martin, eds., *Multiple Paths to Ministry*.

INTRODUCTION

of Theological Schools, the essay suggests that theological education is in a period of change that is currently most evident among mainline Protestant theological schools. Many of these schools were among the first theological schools founded in the United States, he notes. Consequently, many of these experienced growth through the years and have gone on to make significant contributions to theology and to the way in which theological education is carried out both here in the United States and around the world. Greatly impacted by recent changes in the Protestant churches and in the US sociocultural scene, however, these schools have experienced the greatest decline in enrollment and more financial stress than evangelical Protestant or Roman Catholic schools. After his survey and analysis of the wider forces that are influencing religion and theological education, Aleshire argues that the future missions of these schools will require them to make changes in academic policies, educational practices, and facilities to ensure sustainable affordability and to accommodate changing expectations of students and others. Perhaps most importantly, he notes, these schools will need to develop a more formational model of theological education the better to address both the changes that have occurred in the mainline Protestant churches and the needs that these changes have engendered within them.

In the second essay, "America's Changing Religious and Cultural Landscape and Its Implications for Theological Education," Nancy Ammerman looks at changes in American culture that have made the very notion of religious communities and religious leadership an increasing challenge. Similar to Daniel Aleshire, Ammerman believes that the mission of theological schools is closely tied to the education and formation of religious leaders for work in religious communities or congregations. She believes, however, that the education of these potential religious leaders needs to prepare them for congregational settings that have experienced much change in the last four or five decades. Gathering, sustaining, and leading a congregation today requires different assumptions and skills than the ones most theological schools tend to have in mind and are primed to dispense. Today's culture makes it exceedingly difficult to get people in the door of any religious organization, and the unsettledness of all our connections is hard soil in which to grow any sort of community. These are difficult challenges theological schools must help their students to understand and to address, Ammerman suggests. She believes, however, that an important realization can encourage theological schools and their students: despite the challenges, the things that happen in local congregations are more important than ever—to the individuals in them, to the larger society in which we all live, and to the faith traditions in which theological educators participate.

My essay, "Embracing a Greater, Higher Calling: Redefining the Mission and Purpose of the Freestanding Protestant Seminary," also explores some of the different struggles that mainline Protestant theological schools face today and the broader sociocultural and ecclesiastical changes that have contributed to these. But from here the essay goes in a different direction and chooses to focus on a long-standing, ingrained tendency that has impaired the prosperity or good fortune of seminaries: the instinctive assumption that the ultimate and often sole purpose of theological education is to train people for ordained or professional ministry, and specifically for pastoral ministry in a congregation. There may have been a time, many decades ago, when freestanding Protestant seminaries could get by with such a narrow focus and sense of purpose. But times and circumstances have changed. And seminaries must be willing to adopt a wider, deeper, grander understanding of the task of theology and the mission of a seminary. Seminaries need to make room for a greater (dare we say higher?) calling—a calling that includes not only the pursuit of and preparation for ministry but also the fostering of other "professions" and pursuits aimed at the search for transcendence and the building of a more sacred, compassionate, just, and peaceful world. The essay explains why this is so, while also throwing light upon some paths that seminaries can pursue in their attempt to live into this grander calling.

The fourth essay of the book, titled "A House Built on Sand? A Blunt Look at the Assumptions of Theological Education," is a candid, critical, and frankly gloomy assessment of mainline Protestant

INTRODUCTION

theological schools. Written by Nick Carter, erstwhile president of two free-standing seminaries and former private sector executive, this essay lambasts the broken, out-of-touch, and outdated business model of most free-standing seminaries. Claiming that these seminaries can no longer afford to "do business as usual," and that they will need to overcome their aversion to creative change and/or reinvention and to rethink their undergirding core business model, Carter calls for nothing less than a "Cirque de Soleil type response for an industry that has mostly been mired in a Barnum and Bailey world."

The fifth essay tells the story of how Meadville Lombard Theological School, a Unitarian Universalist seminary, overcame the common problem found in denominational seminaries of resistance to institutional change and moved from near death to new life. Titled "From Resistance to Resurrection: Meadville Lombard's Touch Point Model of Theological Education," and co-authored by Sharon Welch and Michael Hogue, it demonstrates how this school embraced contemporary social and cultural changes as catalysts of, rather than as impediments to, theological enrichment and the empowerment of new religious leaders.

The sixth essay, by Dale Irvin, titled "A Reform Amounting to a Revolution: New York Theological Seminary and Theological Education for the City," tells the story of New York Theological Seminary and its evolving commitment to a model of theological education that is *urbancentric*. Irvin highlights the growing global reality of urbanization and explores some of the implications of this for the future of theological education, specifically that the growing cosmopolitan experience of city can be, and perhaps even should be, a central factor in the shaping of the life and curriculum of theological schools today.

Willie Jennings's essay, "The Change We Need: Race and Ethnicity in Theological Education," suggests that the presence of people of color in significant numbers in predominantly white theological institutions has placed a new set of dynamics in the midst of 1) academic theological conversation; 2) the teaching of the subject matter of theological education; and 3) the formation

INTRODUCTION

process of students. Jennings believes that we are only beginning to assess the cost of adaptation for both theological institutions and for scholars of color. The question now is whether institutions will move beyond a facile management of diversity to a productive embodiment of diversity in their educational processes and their common life.

In the book's final essay, "Why Seminaries and the Churches Should Welcome Religious Diversity in the USA," Heidi Hadsell explores the subject of religious diversity and interfaith study in theological education. Acknowledging the likelihood of continuing increases in immigration and mass migration here in the US and around the world, and, therefore, the likely increase in our encounters with religious diversity, Hadsell makes a case for the inclusion of interfaith studies as an integral component of contemporary theological education. To begin with, Hadsell refreshingly shifts the conversation away from the framing of religious diversity in terms of an issue or problem to be managed and towards the envisioning of the increasing encountering of religious diversity as an opportunity for educational, moral, and even faithful or doctrinal enrichment and deepening. Building upon her experience at Hartford Seminary, she argues for a model of integrated education in interfaith studies. This model or approach to interfaith studies emphasizes regular encounter with students, practitioners, and faculty members or teachers of other religious traditions in the classroom. Hadsell ends her essay with a listing of the benefits that can result from engagement in this form of interfaith education in the seminaries and even in the churches.

These essays clearly do not address every possible aspect, issue, perspective, and/or concern related to the enterprise of theological education in the contemporary scene. But they do tackle some of the more important issues and topics connected to this subject matter. Just the same, it should be apparent that it wasn't the intent of the book to present a unified voice or vision on such things as the purpose and mission of theological education; the content of theological education or the way in which it ought to be carried out; or even on the very question of the present state and future prospect of mainline Protestant or mainline denominational theological education in the United States. The truth is that the essays in this book are different in tone and approach. They also convey varied perspectives on these potential questions, and assume different things and postures. Moreover, some of the essays are more critical than others in their assessment of the way in which theological education has often been conceived and carried out.

Yet the essays do all assume that change is in the air in the churches, in the academy, and in the general society, and that theological schools must evolve if they are to survive and even to thrive. Each essay in its own way hopes that mainline US Protestant and/or US mainline denominational theological schools will be able to figure out what the shape, form, methods, and calling or purpose of theological education can or should be in the twenty-first century. Even the most candid, critical, and skeptical of the essays in this book dares to remain hopeful that not only mainline theological education but also that many of the kinds of schools I have mentioned will undergo change and renewal, and find ways to remain alive, relevant, meaningful, and generative. The operative word here is *hopeful*, since it is not optimism or unmitigated expectancy that I sense in these essays. Indeed, the critical assessments, proposals, and case study narratives in the book are meant to stimulate this evolution and movement forward. In this sense, each of the essays wrestles with the challenging present state of mainline Protestant and/or mainline denominational theological education while trying to look forward with hope for better days ahead.

As contributors to this volume, our hope is that our ruminations will serve as an impetus for further dialogue about the present state and possible future of theological education.

Bibliography

Aleshire, Daniel O. *Earthen Vessels: Hopeful Reflections on the Work and Future of Theological Schools*. Grand Rapids: Eerdmans, 2008.

Introduction

Barker, Lance, and B. Edmon Martin, eds. *Multiple Paths to Ministry: New Models for Theological Education*. Cleveland, OH: Pilgrim, 2004.
Chaves, Mark. *American Religion: Contemporary Trends*. Princeton, NJ: Princeton University Press, 2011.
Farley, Edward. *Theologia: The Fragmentation and Unity of Theological Education*. Philadelphia: Fortress, 1983.
Gonzalez, Justo L. *The History of Theological Education*. Nashville: Abingdon, 2015.
Jones, L. Gregory, and Stephanie Paulsell, eds. *The Scope of Our Art: The Vocation of the Theological Teacher*. Grand Rapids: Eerdmans, 2002.
Kelsey, David H. *Between Athens and Berlin: The Theological Education Debate*. Grand Rapids: Eerdmans, 1993.
———. *To Understand God Truly: What's Theological About a Theological School*. Louisville: Westminster John Knox, 1992.
Messer, Donald E. *Calling Church & Seminary into the 21st Century*. Nashville: Abingdon, 1995.

1

First But Not Finished
Mainline Protestant Theological Education

DANIEL O. ALESHIRE

IT WAS AS COMPELLING a day as I have spent in almost thirty years of work with the Association of Theological Schools. I had been invited to give the commencement address at Bangor Theological Seminary. It was the seminary's 199th commencement and its last. A seminary that had faithfully and innovatively served New England congregations for almost 200 years was ceasing to be a degree-granting institution. A school that had survived the Civil War and World War I, the Great Depression and World War II, could not survive the pressures and forces influencing theological schools in the early twenty-first century. The professor whom students had chosen to preach the baccalaureate service that preceded commencement used the call of Abram in Genesis 12 as her text: "Go from your country and your kindred and your father's house to the land that I will show you." The preacher rightly noted that the word translated as "go" is also translated as "leave" and explicated with tenderness and care the difference between leaving a place and going to a new place. "Leaving" can convey a sense of loss of what has passed, while "going" can evoke hope about the future. In many ways, the seminary was leaving 200 years of educating students and granting degrees, while the students—like the graduates in the preceding 198 commencements—were going to something.

Something unique is happening to theological schools as the twenty-first century approaches its third decade. Since World War II, the story of American Protestant theological education has been quite predictable: enrollment grew most years, and slight declines that occurred occasionally were erased by increases in subsequent years. The story changed a decade ago when enrollment began to decline and has continued to decline.

Something is happening, and it is not clear whether theological schools are going somewhere they have never been that holds great promise or if they are leaving a land of kindred and houses for a future of diminished possibilities. Whatever is currently happening is affecting Protestant schools more than Roman Catholic schools, and among Protestants, it is affecting mainline Protestant schools to a much greater extent than it is evangelical schools. Figure 1 shows the enrollment[1] across twenty-five years of mainline Protestant[2] and evangelical Protestant[3] schools in the United States

1. This chapter uses data collected by the ATS Commission on Accrediting from schools that are members of the Association of Theological schools. These data include all schools in the ATS membership, but not theological schools that are not ATS members.

2. Four groups of schools comprise "mainline" in the ATS classification of this ecclesial group. They include (1) the divinity schools of several research universities that do not have a direct denominational connection (Harvard, Yale, Chicago, Vanderbilt); (2) the schools associated with denominations typically classified as mainline Protestant because of their membership in the National Council of Churches and theological position (United Church of Christ, United Methodist Church, Evangelical Lutheran Church in America, Christian Church (Disciples of Christ), Presbyterian Church (USA), The Episcopal Church, some seminaries affiliated with the American Baptist Churches, USA, and the Reformed Church in America); (3) historically black theological schools; and (4) several schools related to the historic Peace churches, the Unitarian Universalist Association, and nondenominational freestanding schools like Union Theological Seminary in New York.

3. ATS assigns a classification to member schools as evangelical, mainline, or Roman Catholic/Orthodox. Although these categories are not exhaustive, most ATS schools fit in one of these categories better than any other. While

that were members of ATS in 1991. Enrollment has declined in the past decade for this common set of schools, but it has declined significantly more in mainline schools. Mainline schools reported an enrollment decline of almost 24 percent from 2005 to 2015, while evangelical schools reported a 6 percent decline during this same time period. Mainline schools' enrollment also declined as a percentage of total US Protestant enrollment over the past twenty-five years. In 1991, mainline schools enrolled 41 percent of all students enrolled in Protestant schools, and by 2015 it had dropped to 29 percent.

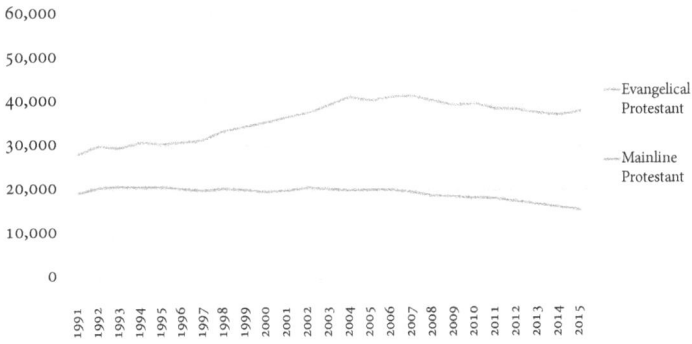

FIGURE 1
Headcount Enrollment in U.S. Evangelical and Mainline Protestant Schools that were ATS Members in 1991
Source: ATS Commission on Accrediting database

This decline is not news. It is felt in schools, and they are busy designing new programs, revising degree requirements, and seeking to respond in other ways to a reality they know all too well. While data from the past decades do not necessarily predict future realities, these data likely convey underlying forces in American Protestantism, not merely a declining number of students who are choosing to pursue theological education.

---

agreement exists about what constitutes mainline Protestant, less agreement exists about what constitutes evangelical Protestant. ATS classifies schools as evangelical if their president or chief executive officer maintains membership in the Fellowship of Evangelical Seminary Presidents, an association not affiliated with ATS, or the school identifies itself as evangelical in its self-description.

The enrollment decline is not the only indicator that something is happening. Freestanding ATS member schools continue to function in the context of significant financial stress. If spending from endowment is controlled to a sustainable 5 percent, approximately 56 percent of mainline Protestant schools operated at a deficit in the most recent year for which complete data are available, and 21 percent operated at a serious deficit (more than $1 million). The data indicate some improvement since 2009, the year that the results of the "great recession" first were evident in annual reports from ATS member schools, but more than half of all freestanding US mainline schools still had deficit operating results in the most recent year. These deficits have often been funded by drawing on endowment resources at a rate greater than a sustainable 5 percent, and years of overspending have diminished the purchasing power of the remaining endowment, which compounds the financial stress.

Financial stress is not news, just as enrollment decline is not news. These two are related, most especially as indicators of stress in the constituency that supplies students, receives graduates, and provides resources for theological education—and that is the equally well-known story of membership decline among mainline Protestant denominations.

While there are several common story lines, these schools share more differences than similarities. They include all of the oldest seminaries, some of the richest schools in terms of endowments or other fiscal assets, and some of the most financially stressed schools. They include university divinity schools, whose faculty are often the pioneers of new knowledge and the agenda setters for other theological research. They also include struggling freestanding schools, whose rich history is not successfully producing a rich, or even adequately resourced, present. Episcopal schools are not like Presbyterian schools, and neither of them is like historically black schools or Unitarian Universalist schools. While there is a defensible common story for mainline schools, it must be constructed from many threads that require as many assumptions as threads. What is true for a group of schools is often not true for any one school. A common story, however, does provide some insight into what is happening in mainline theological schools.

What is happening? While the story can be drawn from many perspectives, I will focus on two: the history of mainline Protestant theological education and cultural forces that are influencing religion and theological education. As best I can tell, these forces are influencing mainline schools in ways they are not affecting Roman Catholic, Orthodox, or evangelical Protestant schools.

Historical Influences on Mainline Protestant schools

Theological schools are founded as religious communities are growing, or as some community of faith has a theological commitment to advance, or as denominations mature and broaden their geographical base. Seminaries are never started as a denomination's last act. As such, whatever contemporary religious commitments are embodied in their current missions, the schools remain historical artifacts of past religious energy. While theological schools change over time, few ever rid themselves of all the DNA that they carry from their founding decades. While the past may not determine the future, its shadow never goes away. William Faulkner wrote that "the past is never dead. It's not even past."[4]

Three waves of founding of theological schools

The majority of schools that are considered mainline Protestant were founded in the nineteenth century and comprise the first wave of development of American theological schools. Before the Revolutionary War, the Protestant ministers who had formal education studied the classical liberal arts curriculum of colonial colleges. After the war, theological education grew by the founding of freestanding seminaries—some of which became freestanding when they separated from colleges and others of which were

4. Padgett, "Requiem for a Nun."

founded as freestanding schools. These new schools were founded by a particular denomination or ecclesial community, educated students exclusively from that constituency, and sent graduates to serve that constituency.

The second wave was the founding of Roman Catholic seminaries in the late nineteenth and early twentieth centuries—as immigration from Ireland, Germany, and southern and eastern Europe brought large numbers of Roman Catholics to the United States. While the oldest seminary in the United States is Roman Catholic,[5] fewer than five Catholic seminaries were in operation prior to 1850. While their structures and degrees were quite different from Protestant schools, these schools clearly represent a second wave of seminary development in North American theological education.

A third wave followed the Modernist-Fundamentalist struggles of the 1920s and advanced significantly after World War II. The vast majority of these post-World-War-II institutions were founded as evangelical denominations grew in the twentieth century, as Asian immigrants either founded or imported denominations that established seminaries in the United States, as communities committed to theological viewpoints established seminaries as a means of advancing those viewpoints, as new expressions of Protestantism like Pentecostalism grew in the twentieth century, and as large congregations extended their ministry through seminary education. More than one-third of the 272 schools that constitute the current membership of the Association of Theological Schools in the United States and Canada (ATS) have been founded since World War II, including some of the largest ATS schools. This third wave also included the invention of the nondenominational seminary. Almost all of the schools established in the first wave were founded by denominations, and all but a few of the Roman Catholic schools that were part of the second wave were founded by dioceses or religious orders. The advent of the nondenominational

---

5. St. Mary's Seminary and University, the diocesan seminary of the Archdiocese of Baltimore, was founded in 1791 by John Carroll, the first US Catholic bishop.

freestanding seminary is an important innovation of twentieth-century theological education.

Among the many influences that history exerts on contemporary theological education, I want to identify three that are particularly important: freestanding denominational schools, the development of specialized theological disciplines, and American denominationalism itself.

The development of freestanding denominational seminaries

When Harvard appointed theological liberal Henry Ware to the Hollis Chair, conservative Calvinist Congregationalists responded by founding Andover Theological Seminary (now Andover Newton Theological School) in 1807. Only a few years later, as Presbyterians were increasingly concerned about the capacity of the church to control the education of its ministers, what is now Princeton Theological Seminary was founded in 1812. The education of Dutch Reformed clergy was separated from what had become Rutgers University when New Brunswick Theological Seminary was formed later in the nineteenth century. The reasons for founding a freestanding theological school varied: for Andover, it was doctrinal controversy; for Princeton, it was church control; for New Brunswick, it was the enlarged educational scope of Rutgers.

This pattern of freestanding theological schools continued through the nineteenth century. The German Reformed Church, for example, established a program for the education of ministers in connection with Dickinson College in 1825 that, later in the century, became Lancaster Theological Seminary. Southern Presbyterians established ministry education in 1812 as an adjunct of Hampden-Sydney College that eventuated in the founding later in the century of what is now Union Presbyterian Theological Seminary.

Other theological schools were established as freestanding institutions from their beginning. The bishops of the Episcopal Church founded The General Theological Seminary in 1817, and

Virginia Episcopalians founded the Protestant Episcopal Theological Seminary (now commonly known as Virginia Theological Seminary) in 1823. Newton Theological Institution was established in Massachusetts for the training of Baptist ministers in 1825, and the first Lutheran seminary in the United States was founded in Gettysburg, Pennsylvania, in 1826.

In the span of a few decades in the early nineteenth century, Congregationalists, Presbyterians, Episcopalians, Baptists, and Lutherans all had seminaries that were independent of other educational institutions and tightly related to a single denomination. The freestanding denominational seminary became the dominant institutional form for the education of ministers for the nineteenth and much of the twentieth centuries.

Specialized theological disciplines

Glenn Miller, the premier historian of American Protestant theological education, argues that freestanding theological schools provided an institutional home for the development of specialized theological disciplines.[6] Before the formation of these schools, theology and Bible were taught primarily as part of a broad curriculum of classical studies. Freestanding schools provided the educational space for different disciplines to develop, and by the end of the nineteenth century, maturing disciplines led to the establishment of scholarly societies like the Society of Biblical Literature and the American Society of Church History, both founded in 1888.

These specialized disciplines developed approaches to the study of Scripture and church history that were more critical and analytical, often resulting in conflict as the assertions and questions raised by critical biblical and historical studies threatened traditional commitments. Charles Briggs at Union Theological Seminary in New York championed the critical study of Scripture, and the ensuing controversy resulted in Union separating itself from Presbyterian control in the 1890s. William Whitsitt, a church historian, was forced from the presidency of The Southern Baptist

---

6. Miller, *Piety and Profession*, particularly chapters 3, 4, 5, and 6.

Theological Seminary in that same decade because he argued that baptism by immersion had not been practiced continuously since the apostolic era—as some Baptists had argued. Over time, the critical study of Scripture and disciplined historical studies won among the schools that are now considered mainline Protestant, and specialized disciplines became the normative structure of the theological curriculum. By the twentieth century, scholarly methods that emerged by contesting orthodoxies of many kinds became the orthodox methodology for the study of Bible, history, and theology.

American denominationalism

Nineteenth-century America was a nation of Presbyterians, Congregationalists, Reformed, Methodists, Episcopalians, Baptists, Lutherans, and adherents to the Stone-Campbell movement, and seminaries were, for the most part, tightly related to denominations. Most schools enrolled only students from the denomination to which the seminary was related; denominational seminaries socialized students into denominationally unique patterns of ministry; and graduates served in the denomination to which their seminary was related. The seminaries were both a part of the denominated structure of American Christianity and a contributor to maintaining that structure.

These separate Protestant communities were competitive with one another, and denominational seminaries likely contributed to the competition. Large social distances were created from small doctrinal differences. Perhaps more than advocating doctrinal differences, denominational schools kept ministry students from different denominations separate from one another. They formed different patterns of socialization to the ministry and cultivated friendship patterns that were more internal to one denomination than external and across denominations. The competitive nature of nineteenth-century Protestantism contributed to numeric growth, and as denominations grew in membership and strength, they founded colleges, children's homes, homes for the aged, hospitals, seminaries, and extensive missionary enterprises. The century ended with a culturally established Protestantism that was ordered by competitive denominational structures that were institutionally robust.

The nineteenth century also ended with the emerging interest among many Protestants for less competitive and more cooperative engagement with one another. A perception was developing that Christian witness and work might be better served by increasing cooperation among denominations and, in its boldest vision, eventual church union. The twentieth-century ecumenical movement did not begin in the seminaries, but mainline theological schools were supportive of it, provided scholarship for its theological underpinnings, and gave leadership to its mid-twentieth-century structures. This more cooperative vision began to influence how mainline schools understood themselves as "denominational" and how they judged the strengths and weaknesses of their denominations.

Historical Influences and the Future

I am not a historian, but I have become increasingly impressed by the power of historical influences on the current reality and future prospects of theological schools. Mainline Protestant theological schools grew to maturity during a historical moment, and that past provides both needed ballast and heavy weight as they find their way into the twenty-first century.

As a group of schools, mainline Protestant seminaries have the oldest average age, and age provides ballast. These schools have the benefit of good reputation and endowments that have accrued over time. While mainline Protestant schools are fewer in number than evangelical Protestant schools, they hold almost three-and-a-half times the endowment of evangelical schools. Mainline denominations enjoyed cultural establishment for all of the nineteenth century and the first part of the twentieth century, and that reality provided privilege and cultural access. Many of these schools have architecturally significant facilities that provided public recognition and contributed to their surrounding communities. Age can also impose weight that makes movement to the future difficult. The habits of prior cultural privilege can linger after the privilege has been withdrawn, which can restrict making the changes that the future requires. Endowments can blunt the impact of forces, like declining enrollment, that need careful attention. Buildings that fit patterns of theological education in the nineteenth and first half of the twentieth century have become burdensome with deferred maintenance in this century. Some architectural icons of a culturally triumphant Protestantism seem anachronistic in this century, given the fundamental changes in mainline Protestantism.

Mainline Protestant schools entered the mid-twentieth century as denominational schools, and, because their identities were wedded to their denominations, at least part of their fates as institutions were tied to the fates of their denominations. Mainline denominations weakened significantly during the last half of the twentieth and first decades of this century, which resulted in a decline in students. Many present-day mainline denominations did not exist when the seminaries were founded. The schools related to the UCC, PCUSA, UMC, and ELCA are older than the denominations with which they now identify, and constituent loyalties from earlier denominational alignments have not always passed to the current denominations. Denominational funding has declined as a percentage of needed revenue for four decades now, and schools have increasingly needed to secure contributions from individuals and begun to depend more heavily on tuition. The consequences of changes in enrollment, funding, and denominational developments, along with ecclesial commitments to cooperative ecumenical theological education, contributed to distancing between many mainline denominational seminaries and their respective denominations. A palpable connection between theological schools and their founding denominations remains, but there is also discernable distance.

With the exception of the Methodist and non-denominational university-related divinity schools, mainline Protestant seminaries sustained the freestanding structure they invented. As special-purpose higher education institutions, they are ideally designed for the education of religious leaders. And, as special-purpose institutions, their future hinges on the special purpose for which they exist. If denominations need fewer ministers in the future, a special-purpose institution for the education of ministers has limited options to enhance its enrollment. While the work of the schools changes as ministry changes, few seminaries have been very successful at extending their educational efforts beyond education of religious professionals or academic education in theological disciplines. The freestanding structure becomes problematic as enrollments decline and the needed administrative infrastructure of graduate-level theological schools expands. According to the data that member schools report to ATS, freestanding schools actually spend more on institutional costs (administration, finance, development, facilities, information technology) than on educational costs (library, faculty, academic administration). One way to attenuate this overall cost structure is to affiliate with a larger educational institution, which some mainline schools have done and others are considering.

Mainline Protestant schools are united in their allegiance to critical scholarship. There is not a Methodist or Presbyterian way to study Scripture; there is a common way to study Scripture that employs critical methodologies. The critical scholarly approaches that came kicking and screaming into the work of these schools in the late nineteenth century now serve as a common glue—an agreed-upon convention in the twenty-first century. The academic guilds that these schools helped form in the nineteenth century have become powerful forces influencing areas of research to be pursued and defining the methods that characterize scholarly credibility. They also provide the context in which scholars gain recognition and provide connections that facilitate moving from one position to another.

In many ways, the institutional framework and scholarly structures of the nineteenth century have considerable influence on present-day mainline Protestant theological education. Schools in this century differ in many ways, but the imprint of the nineteenth century is evident. It does provide ballast in challenging times, but it also provides weight that inhibits the schools' ability to be as nimble and innovative as the current century will require.

Cultural Influences on Mainline Protestant Theological Education

Theological education is situated in the church, in higher education, and in the culture of which both are a part. In addition to the influences that a particular history exerts on theological schools, cultural forces exert their own compelling influence. I have spoken and written about several cultural drivers or influences elsewhere,[7] and in this chapter will focus on the ones that I think have the greatest influence on mainline Protestant theological schools.

The changing social status of religion in American culture

In the first decade of the nineteenth century, church leaders were shaping culture in North America as much as they were leading religion. Joseph Willard, president of Harvard in 1800, came to the university from the pastorate, and his two successors were also clergymen.[8] During the same period, Samuel Smith, a clergyman, was the president of the College of New Jersey (now Princeton University). Benjamin Moore was the Anglican bishop of New York when he became president of what is now Columbia University.[9] Clergy in colonial America and in the first decades of nationhood led more than religious institutions; they contributed significantly to the cultural and intellectual leadership of the nation. Clergy were public intellectuals and civic leaders.

---

7. "Theological Education in the United States," *The Oxford Handbook of Religion and American Education*, in press.
8. www.president.harvard.edu/history/history3.php.
9. www.columbia.edu/cu/president/docs/history/index.html.

In this century, the capacity of contemporary religious leaders to shape culture has dissipated significantly. The broader culture that granted considerable establishment to nineteenth-century Protestantism has rescinded it in this century. Religion has been reassigned from a public good to a private good. Religious leaders in this century are no doubt as talented as early nineteenth-century leaders, but religion does not have the cultural platform on which they can exercise cultural leadership. The culture recognizes religion as a valuable personal choice, but it does not readily grant it a seat at the table where the culture incubates its future. Seminary graduates in the future will make significant contributions to the religious lives and visions of countless individuals and congregations, but they will not wield the kind of influence that Joseph Willard or Samuel Smith did. In this century, religious leaders will exercise public influence primarily through the direct ministry of congregations, the work of individuals who constitute them, and the entities that communities of faith create and support.

This is an especially difficult reality for mainline Protestant schools. Their founders were the culture shapers, and if religion has lost cultural status, mainline Protestants feel the greatest loss. Many scholars in mainline schools have undertaken efforts at public theology, and in an interesting way, these efforts are an indicator of the privilege and access that has been lost. In the nineteenth century, established Protestantism *was* public theology. It is only when the culture distanced religion from the public platform that mainline theologians sensed a need to find a way to exert a public voice.

Mainline Protestants face another loss. Until the last quarter of the twentieth century, mainline denominations were the dominant form of Protestantism, and the conventions of mainline Protestantism defined much of American religion. Today, evangelical Protestants are the dominant form of Protestantism, and their conventions are providing that definition. The change is a function of both the increase in the number of evangelical Protestants and evangelical-leaning mainline Protestants *and* the decline in the number of mainline Protestants. The shifted Protestant center of gravity shows up in theological schools. In 1981–1982, just over 53 percent of all ATS member schools were mainline Protestant and 19 percent were evangelical Protestant. This year, the ATS membership has more evangelical than mainline Protestant schools. Last academic year, evangelical schools enrolled about 62 percent of all students in ATS schools, and mainline schools enrolled about 28 percent.

These losses are not fatal, but they require attention about how work will be done in the future. Mainline schools will not find their way to the future as if they still enjoyed the benefits of cultural establishment when they do not or as if mainline were the dominant form of Protestantism when it is not. The future contribution of mainline Protestant schools begins with a past that actually is over and that will not be reclaimed in the future.

Changing status of higher education

Religion is not the only social institution that has lost cultural privilege. While higher education may have more privilege than religion, it has lost a great deal of the privilege that it had in the nineteenth and much of the twentieth centuries. Questions about access, affordability, and accountability are indicators of this altered status. These are not the questions asked of a privileged institution; they are questions that are asked when an institution is viewed as a functionary of culture and the culture is not sure it is getting what it needs from the function.

In an earlier time, it was an individual citizen's responsibility to *go* to an institution of higher education. My now-deceased father-in-law grew up on a tobacco farm in rural Kentucky. He wanted a higher education degree, and with great determination but little money, left the farm and went to an institution of higher learning. Increasingly, it has become the responsibility of higher education to *come* to students. If my father-in-law were a college freshman today, he would have several higher education options available to him without going anywhere: community college, distance learning programs from a far-away institution, or branch campuses of another institution.

Access is greater than it has ever been, but so is the cost. I went away to college, like my father-in-law, and needed to pay most of my own expenses. I worked several jobs, lived cheaply, and was able to pay tuition at the school I attended. It would be impossible for any student to work part time and pay his or her way at the same institution now—unless he or she was a part-time hedge fund manager! The cost of education has increased more rapidly than the cost of most other sectors in the American economy, and it has contributed to public suspicion about the value of higher education. Not only should higher education be accessible; it should be affordable.

These accessible and affordable institutions are also accountable for demonstrating that they are achieving their educational goals. This accountability extends to multiple constituencies, although it is formalized in accreditation, a process that is increasingly influenced by federal government expectations about the nature of that accountability.

Because theological education is highly enmeshed in the models and practices of higher education, it is dealing with its version of questions about access, affordability, and accountability.

Greater access requires changes in educational practices. Mainline Protestant theological schools have favored educational practices in which students study face-to-face with one another and their professors, worship together, live in proximity to one another, share meals, and otherwise experience communal patterns of education for ministry. These schools have tended to be suspicious of extension education and distance education—practices that would make theological education more accessible—because they did not fit a valuable and cherished educational model. Meanwhile, campuses have become more a place to park the car and run to class than a communal gathering for learning and shared lives of faith. Deans of ATS schools estimated in a 2016 survey that about 25 percent of students live on or near campus.[10] Theological edu-

---

10. These data are from a survey conducted in 2015 as part of the ATS

cation has become significantly more accessible, but it has taken theological schools much longer to develop this accessibility than it has higher education in general, and it has taken mainline Protestant schools longer than it has evangelical Protestant schools.

Affordability is an issue for theological schools. Funding provided by denominations in an earlier era subsidized much of the cost of theological education. That funding has dissipated, and its replacement has come from endowments, individual donors, and tuition. Mainline schools, with the help of their endowments, return about 50 percent of tuition charges to students in the form of tuition remission and scholarships. (Evangelical Protestant schools, by contrast, return about 25 percent to students.) Even with the generous subsidy that mainline schools provide, students are paying an ever-increasing share of institutional costs in the form of tuition, and to fund tuition and living expenses, students are borrowing money. More mainline seminary students are taking out loans, and the average amount of those loans is larger than for students in ATS schools as a whole. According to ATS data, about 56 percent of students who graduated in 2016 had incurred debt to pay for their theological education, and of students who borrowed, the average total of seminary debt was approximately $36,800. For students in mainline Protestant schools, the numbers are about 10 percent higher—62 percent of students incur debt, and the average of seminary educational debt is $39,500.[11]

If mainline schools provide a higher percentage of aid to their students than do evangelical schools, why do more students at mainline schools graduate with debt that is higher than the average for all students in ATS? While no one answer is possible, several factors may contribute. Tuition at mainline schools is actually higher than it is at evangelical Protestant schools. However, from its work on the Economic Challenges Facing Future

---

Educational Models and Practices project.

11. These data are taken from the Graduating Student Questionnaire (GSQ), administered by ATS and completed by graduates from more than half of all ATS schools. The GSQ data compares favorably to other studies of student debt that were based on analysis of individual financial aid transcripts.

Ministers project (a project coordinating the work of more than 60 ATS schools with grants from Lilly Endowment to help students increase financial literacy and minimize debt), ATS has learned that the amount of tuition does not correlate positively with the amount of debt. Seminary students appear to be using much of the funds they borrow for living expenses, and the reticence of many mainline schools to utilize educational practices like extension education and distance learning may force more students to relocate to undertake their theological education, which contributes to increased debt. ATS data also indicate that African American students have higher debt levels than do other groups of students, and as you will see in the next section, mainline schools have a significantly higher percentage of African American students than do ATS schools as a whole. It is not clear if these are the real reasons, but graduates' debt is a significant issue in all of theological education, most especially in mainline Protestant theological schools. As membership declines congregation by congregation, and the chances for adequate compensation and ministerial career development are constrained, some mainline denominations are asking if it is just to require or even encourage someone to undertake several years of theological education that require incurring debt. Mainline Protestant denominations have been the epicenter for advocating for a learned ministry, but there is less clarity about the affordability of a learned ministry in the future.

Accountability is a diverse responsibility for theological schools. They are formally accountable to accrediting agencies, but more importantly, they are accountable to the constituencies they serve: the donors who increasingly provide necessary funding, students who are paying or borrowing to pay for their theological education, and the denominations and congregations in which graduates will serve. While some constituencies are readily identifiable, others are more elusive. A significant percentage of mainline seminary graduates minister in denominations with which the seminary has no meaningful contact or association. An increasing percentage of graduates are choosing to serve in areas of work that are quite different from the ones to which the seminary orders its educational efforts. Accountability has moved from a relatively homogeneous pattern to more diverse and complex patterns.

Fundamental shift in the US population

By 2040 the American population will have completed a fundamental shift that began in the late nineteenth century: a nation of immigrants largely from Europe, Ireland, and Great Britain will be a nation in which "white" will be the racial minority.[12] By mid-century, if not before, persons of African, Asian, and Hispanic descent will outnumber white residents. The America that was the new world of Europe will become the new world of the world. This is a huge change, and no liberal democracy has ever gone through this kind of change. This chapter is being written during a presidential race in which new immigrant communities figure prominently— as a source of voters for one candidate and as a source of anger and rage for the other candidate. This change in the racial composition of the population will not come about quietly in communities, in the nation, or in religion. Communities of faith that are unable to become culturally and racially amphibious will decline, and those that succeed in this fundamental cultural capacity will thrive.

Historically white mainline Protestant theological schools are now more racially inclusive than the denominations to which they are related. These schools have advocated aggressively for racial justice and have taken on issues of white privilege, racism, and racial prejudice so effectively that few students graduate from mainline schools without being exposed to them. The capacity of theological schools to address this changed population depends, in part, on the percentage of students from racial/ethnic communities and the percentage of faculty from racial/ethnic communities.

The past thirty years have witnessed significant change in the racial composition of students in all ATS member schools. In 1981–1982, African, Asian, and Hispanic-descent students

---

12. A good analysis of population trends, extracted from US census and other data sources, can be found at U.S. Population Projections: 2005–2050, http//pewsocialtrends.org/2008/02/11/us-population-projections-2005-2050/.

accounted for 8 percent of total enrollment. This past academic year, these students, along with visa students, constituted 37 percent of total enrollment. Figure 2 shows the percentage of enrollment in mainline and evangelical Protestant theological schools by racial/ethnic groups for the 2015–2016 academic year. While evangelical and mainline schools both have the same percentage of racial/ethnic students (41 percent), the composition of students of color varies. Half of all students of color in mainline schools are African American, comprising 20 percent of total enrollment. The percentage of African Americans is even greater if historically black theological schools (which ATS classifies as mainline) are included. Mainline schools have significantly fewer Asians and visa students than do evangelical schools, and slightly fewer Hispanic/Latino/a students. The distribution among African descent, Hispanic/Latino/a descent, and Asian descent is more even among evangelical schools. In both mainline and evangelical Protestant schools, the percentage of racial/ethnic students has increased each year across the past two decades, which is a function of the combination of a decreasing number of white students and an increasing number of students of color

FIGURE 2
Enrollment by Race/Ethnicity
in U.S. Protestant Theological Schools, Fall 2015

	Evangelical	Mainline
American Indian, Alaskan Native or Inuit	1%	1%
Asian or Pacific Islander	10%	4%
Black Non-Hispanic	11%	20%
Hispanic	7%	6%
Multiracial	1%	2%
Visa or Nonresident Alien	11%	8%
White Non-Hispanic	59%	59%

Source: ATS Commission on Accrediting database
Note: This excludes the six historically black theological schools.

Mainline schools have been more successful than have evangelical schools in recruiting faculty of color, as Figure 3 indicates.

The faculty of mainline schools is 27 percent persons of color, of whom the majority are of African descent. The faculty of evangelical Protestant schools is 18 percent persons of color, of whom the majority are of Asian descent. In some ways, all theological schools are ahead of their denominations in terms of the percentage of racial/ethnic constituents, which is exactly where they should be to prepare students for the population changes that are already evident and will be more pronounced in coming decades.

FIGURE 3
Faculty by Race/Ethnicity
in U.S. ATS Protestant Schools, Fall 2015

	Evangelical	Mainline
American Indian, Alaskan Native or Inuit	0%	0%
Asian or Pacific Islander	9%	7%
Black Non-Hispanic	5%	14%
Hispanic	3%	5%
Multiracial	0%	0%
Visa or Nonresident Alien	1%	1%
White Non-Hispanic	82%	73%

Source: ATS Commission on Accrediting database
Note: This excludes the six historically black theological schools.

Cultural influences and the future

Together, these cultural influencers provide both assets and liabilities for mainline Protestant schools. Like historical influences, these factors are not determinative, but they are influential. Theological schools in the United States are currently at a transformational moment. I have joked that, while schools have often seen their educational mission as transforming students or their prophetic mission as transforming the church or society, they don't particularly like to be transformed themselves. The schools, however, don't have a choice: much has changed, and much more will change. How might mainline schools negotiate the future?

Looking Forward with Hope

The Future of Mainline Protestant Theological Education

Predicting anything is risky, but if schools are to look thoughtfully to the future, they need some hunches. All of theological education is in a period of substantive change, and the result of that change will not be a linear extension of what has been in the past. Theological education will likely change more in form and practice in the next two decades than it has in the past several decades combined. The result will be far more diversity in educational practices and institutional structures. Some schools will do their work in the future essentially the same way they are doing it now. Other schools will do their work in essentially the same ways they are doing it now but with recognizable improvements over current practices. Still other schools will do theological education in ways that are very different from current practices. Some schools will merge with other schools to continue and strengthen their missions. Some will close because their mission is completed and constituency dissipated. Some new schools will be founded. Theological schools simply will not travel one road to the future. In a decade or two in the future, parts of theological education will have such different faces that some people will look at them and ask "Is this really theological education?"

Across the past decade, the images that Ronald Heifetz[13] has introduced have become as common among theological school leaders as the Myers-Briggs Type Indicator or the Enneagram. Even if overused, they remain instructive. Heifetz argues that organizations make two kinds of changes in the context of the changing realities in which they do their work. The first is technical change—the kind of change that helps an existing structure adjust to a new set of circumstances so it functions better. The second is adaptive change—the kind of change in which the organization does something truly different in the face of changing circumstances. Technical change is not easy, but it is easier than adaptive change. Technical change refines and adjusts institutional

---

13. Heifetz, *Leadership without Easy Answers*.

efforts, and adaptive change alters them in fundamental ways. Both require considerable effort, and my hunch is that both will be necessary as theological schools move into the future.

The technical changes: academic excellence without privilege

Mainline theological education has benefited from cultural and religious privilege that has made certain academic practices possible and enhanced them over time. The future will require schools to push toward academic excellence absent the privilege that supported those practices in an earlier era, and that will require technical changes in four valuable academic practices: the prophetic role of the theological professor, tenure, disciplinary specialization, and teaching practices.

Prophetic role. An ethnographic study of two theological schools, now decades old, found that both schools, one mainline and the other evangelical Protestant, had a "central message" or "normative goal." For the mainline seminary, the central message was about the reform of Christian and social life. "Redeeming grace becomes available as prejudices are changed and unjust structures are replaced with others that require the inclusion and equal treatment of all."[14] This research effort studied only one mainline school, and what was true of it may not be true of others. Over my years of working with theological schools, however, the commitment of that single mainline school seems evident in many others. Many faculty in mainline theological schools contend that an important part of their work is speaking the truth to unjust powers and structures, and that a central goal of theological education is to help students understand that redeeming unjust social structures is a primary goal of the Christian project. Not all faculty in mainline schools think their role is prophetic or that the seminary's central goal should focus on social change, but many do, and this conviction constitutes a considerable strength of mainline

14. Carroll et al., *Being There*, 205.

theological education. Even faculty who may not agree that social change should be the primary educational agenda would agree that a world that is less racist, sexist, heterosexist, and homophobic in attitudes, and less colonial and oppressive in structures, would be more truly Christian.

A primary strategy for advocating this kind of world has been theological faculty members speaking prophetically to the systems and structures most in need of reform. This role is threatened by the disinclination or inability of the culture to hear them. In a way, the prophetic witness of mainline theological schools has its roots both in an understanding of the gospel and in the cultural privilege that, at an earlier time, granted greater access to the structures that influence culture. That privilege provided cultural listeners. As recently as the mid-twentieth century, when Reinhold Niebuhr was pictured on the front page of a national news magazine,[15] the culture still seemed to be listening. It appears different now. In 2016, *Washington Post* commentator E. J. Dionne asked, "Over the past several decades, those who view religion with respect regularly come back to the same question: What has happened to the religious intellectuals, the thinkers taken seriously by nonbelievers as well as believers?" He continued, "In this increasingly secular time, a natural follow-up question ratifies the point of the original query: Who cares? Why should the thinking of those inspired by faith even matter to those who don't share it?"[16] Dionne goes on to argue that this culture should be listening to religious voices. It does not appear, however, to be inclined to do so. People are speaking convincingly, but it is less clear if the culture is listening attentively. Are mainline prophet professors like street preachers with sandwich signs declaring the dangers of hell as people walk by with well-honed inattention? How does the prophet declare the needed judgment if no one is listening except other professor-prophets who agree with the judgment? Prophetic witness in the future will need to find a way to gain cultural attention.

15. *Time*, US Edition, March 8, 1948.

16. https://www.washingtonpost.com/opinions/in-search-of-humble-prophets/2016/08/24/7fa00d86-6a0e-11e6-ba32-5a4bf5aad4fa_story.html.

Tenure. More faculty of mainline schools enjoy the benefits of academic tenure than do the faculties of evangelical and Roman Catholic schools. While about two-thirds of the ATS schools have policies that provide tenure, virtually all mainline schools have these policies. Tenure is a historic academic practice and is policy at every research university in the United States and Canada, as well as in most other institutions of higher education. Tenure is typically granted by a governing board only after the tenured faculty of the institution have evaluated a candidate and recommended that tenure be granted. As such, professors with tenure exercise considerable power over the shape and future of the faculty. Tenure is a structure of considerable power and privilege. It is an interesting conundrum that faculty benefit from a system of academic power and privilege to speak truth to other powers and privileges.

Fewer schools in the future will offer tenure. This is not due to a lessened sense of its social value or contribution to academic quality. Tenure will become a victim of relentless financial stress in schools and changes in cultural perceptions about higher education. Tenure policies and practices were generally established when a mandatory retirement age was legal. Because a school granted tenure to a forty-year-old professor who would be required to retire at sixty-five, it could assess the duration and economic impact of granting tenure. With mandatory retirement policies now illegal, tenure guarantees employment for an indefinite future, and an indefinite future means an undeterminable cost. Competent professorial work should be encouraged to continue as long as the competency is present, but determining incompetence in faculty work can be very difficult legally and, in the small and often familial faculties of ATS member schools, even more difficult interpersonally. Senior tenured faculty tend to be, and rightfully deserve to be, at the top of the pay scale, and as long as they continue to teach, they increase the overall cost of theological education.

Cost is a big issue for financially stressed theological schools. The combination of financial stress and the unpredictable cost of granting tenure will push financially stressed schools to revise or eliminate tenure policies in the future—not because it is less valued as an academic practice but because it becomes unaffordable. Tenure will continue to be an important part of theological education, but it likely will be an indicator as much of institutional wealth as of academic excellence.

Schools can address the cost of instruction in other ways. While higher education in general has moved aggressively in its use of part-time, adjunct, and contingent faculty, theological schools have not done this. The percentage of part-time faculty for ATS schools has been relatively stable over the past decade. If ATS schools keep a large percentage of full-time faculty, the future may well occasion the greater use of contract full-time faculty than of tenured or tenurable faculty. Academic excellence can still be achieved, as is evident in the one-third of ATS schools that do not grant tenure. One technical change that many mainline schools may need to make in the coming decades will involve faculty policies that assure continuity of a professoriate, protections for freedom of inquiry, and sustainable affordability.

Broader disciplinary structures. The trajectory of knowledge in any area of academic endeavor has only one direction—growth and expansion—and the academic strategy for dealing with the increasing volume of information is specialization. During the past century, for example, a New Testament professor's domain of expertise has moved from the Testament as a whole to Synoptic, Johannine, or Pauline scholarship, further divided by more narrow areas of expertise, such as feminist or post-colonial thought. As it becomes less possible for one person to know all of the corpus of a discipline, the typical response of the academy is to increase the number of faculty in an area, each holding particular expertise in a different part of the discipline. The growth is not limited to disciplinary specialization; it also includes the introduction of new and needed disciplinary approaches to theological education.

While disciplinary information will continue to expand, and the complexity of ministerial practice increase, the financial constraints of most theological schools will prohibit increasing the size of the faculty to accommodate these developments. Some will be able to afford faculty with increased specializations; most will not. This reality will precipitate a new intellectual demand on faculty and theological curricula: the construction of intellectually sophisticated, broader disciplinary areas. While a significant approach in contemporary intellectual effort questions anything resembling a grand narrative, the future of theological education will require the development of narratives of study that are more integrative and holistic. Schools may return to an earlier pattern of theological faculty work in which each professor was responsible for a broad range of "the body of divinity." The result will be a new kind of disciplinary structure and the scholarly competence needed to work with broadened categories in an intellectual age that is suspicious of grand narratives. This is a technical change that will require the theological schools that invented the current disciplinary structure to reinvent it.

Teaching practices. Theological education practices were relatively homogeneous across much of the twentieth century. Most schools conducted on-site, face-to-face classes, and the MDiv curriculum tended to have three somewhat equal areas of study: Scripture and biblical languages; theology, philosophy, ethics, and history; and a wide range of pastoral arts/practical theology. Educational practices began to change in the 1980s, educational diversity emerged more broadly in the early 2000s, and it will expand even more in the coming decade. The diversity will be both in educational practices and in curricular strategy. The ATS Commission on Accrediting approved the first extension site to grant the MDiv fewer than twenty-five years ago. It approved the possibility of offering courses by distance education for the first time in 2000. Today, degree-granting extension sites, branch campuses, distance education, and courses offered in brief intensive sessions are normative.

Mainline schools have been slower to implement these newer educational strategies—a reluctance that has been partly a function of the cushion of cultural establishment, external ordination requirements by their churches, and sufficient endowment to pay increasingly expensive bills. The cushion is evaporating or gone for many mainline schools. As the denominations to which mainline schools are related continue to change, and likely experience continued decline in numbers, pressure will mount for these schools to develop alternative educational strategies. Many are diversifying their educational programs and structures, but far more will need to be done in the future.

Not all schools will change their educational strategies. Some will continue to have students on campus in face-to-face courses in proximity to a library with its multiple resources. This kind of educational practice, however, will be as much an indicator of institutional wealth as it is of educational commitment. Mainline schools are diversifying educationally and will continue to do so in the future. These changes in educational practices are, once again, technical changes, and the knowledge and expertise necessary for these changes is readily available among theological educators.

Facilities and institutional form. Many mainline schools have campuses built for the pattern of education that include housing and food service facilities in addition to library, classroom, common gathering spaces, and offices. As educational practices have changed, some of these facilities become as unnecessary as they are unaffordable. In addition to their usefulness, the elegance of older buildings becomes a deferred maintenance burden as they age. Buildings, even unnecessary ones, are often institutional icons and symbols of stability and capacity. While selling or repurposing facilities often constitute difficult decisions for freestanding seminary boards, many schools have made substantial decisions about facilities, and many more will. The campus of the future will not look like the campus of the past.

Mainline schools have held onto the freestanding institutional model they invented, and that model is succumbing to economic realities that make it increasingly difficult to sustain smaller, freestanding schools. The era of the mom-and-pop style of administration has passed; administrative structures increasingly need to be expert and robust; the necessary indirect costs of maintaining a modern graduate school consume a significant part of institutional budgets. Many former freestanding schools have merged with another educational institution, and others likely will do so in the future. Once again, these are technical changes. They involve difficult decisions that result in very complicated implementation efforts, but in the end, they are technical changes. They make current patterns of education more affordable but do not fundamentally alter the educational practices or goals.

The adaptive change: formational theological education

One change that may emerge over the next few decades is truly adaptive, as defined in the Heifetz categories, and will involve the shift from the professional model of theological education to a more formational model. The changes in theological education that grew to their full maturity after World War II established theological education as professional education. It became less important for educated clergy to know Cicero or Homer, as had been the case in the early nineteenth century, and more important that they knew biblical and theological disciplines and had the ability to administer a congregation, to guide educational, mission, and service programs; to counsel parishioners; to assess community and congregational needs; and to preach effectively—especially to preach effectively. Protestant ministry was never fully understood as a profession like law or medicine, but the model of professional education became the dominant pattern by which church professionals were educated.

I think that the professional model is receding and a formational model of theological education is slowly emerging. In theological schools, a new model of education never fully replaces an older model; these schools change by addition, like a tree grows by adding new rings, and the old seldom goes away altogether. The result is that transition is subtle and murky and does not become clear until the future has become a distant past. In the current professional model, formational educational practices are present, but in a subordinate role. Over time, these formational aspects that have been in the background will assume an increasingly dominant role. Skills and knowledge will continue to be crucial, but they will become increasingly insufficient in and of themselves. In an age of diminishing cultural influence of the church and increasing secularity of the culture at large, the integrity of religious leadership will increasingly depend on authentic religious commitment and maturity.

The ATS accrediting standards adopted in 1996 hint at the role of personal and spiritual maturity. The standard states: "In a theological school, the overarching goal is the development of theological understanding, that is, aptitude for theological reflection and wisdom pertaining to responsible life in faith. Comprehended in this overarching goal are others such as deepening spiritual awareness, growing in moral sensibility and character, gaining an intellectual grasp of the tradition of the faith community, and acquiring the abilities requisite to the exercise of ministry in that community."[17] Formational theological education includes educating for an intellectual grasp of the theological disciplines and competent pastoral skills, but it undertakes this work with careful attention to authentic humanity, relational ability, and spiritual maturity. In the study of the education for the professions conducted by the Carnegie Foundation a decade ago, formative education was identified as central to the education of clergy—its most unique characteristic when compared to education for other professions that have become more beholden to forms of technical rationalism in their educational approaches.[18] Greg Jones and Kevin Armstrong argue that, "insofar as (theological schools) are preparing people for Christian pastoral ministry, they are necessarily involved in formation as well as education, in shaping character as well as conveying content and patterns of thinking, in nurturing holiness as well as equipping people with skills."[19]

Mainline Protestant theological education has been deeply embedded in the professional model of theological education. If

---

17. ATS Commission on Accrediting Standards, http://www.ats.edu/uploads/accrediting/documents/general-institutional-standards.pdf, 3.1.

18. Foster et al., *Educating Clergy*. See especially the introduction written by William Sullivan, 8–12.

19. Jones and Armstrong, *Resurrecting Excellence*, 121.

I am right about a future in which theological education is more formational, mainline schools will have substantive adjustments to make. These schools have a long history of constructing learned ministry from critical reflection and academic learning of theological disciplines. The adjustment to a "formed" ministry may be difficult, especially if it is perceived as being less intellectually rigorous than the current model. Whatever it may be, however, formational theological education dare not be intellectually vacuous. It needs singular intellectual attention, and mainline theological educators will need to identify the characteristics of mature, intellectually informed, spirituality that are faithful to the long traditions of mainline Protestantism. An important key to this effort might be the argument that Edward Farley advanced that theological education should attend to sapiential learning far more than to a clerical paradigm—by which he meant something very similar to what I have been calling the professional model.[20]

While formational education will use many of the educational resources employed in current theological education, it will require other educational interventions. Mainline schools have already been inventing new educational strategies in efforts regarding racism, white privilege, and racial justice. Many mainline schools want graduates who understand structural racism and white privilege and who *have dealt with their own* prejudice. These two educational goals require different educational strategies: understanding can be achieved by traditional academic strategies, but dealing with students' own privilege and racism involves confrontation, reflection on fundamental aspects of personhood, and emotive forms of learning. This second set of practices comprise formational patterns of education that deal with character and spirituality.

If a more formational pattern of theological education does emerge into greater dominance, mainline seminaries will need to do two things to embrace the future. The first is to discern intellectually viable ways of understanding spiritual, moral, and personal maturity that constitute an acceptable goal for theological

20. Farley, *Theologia*.

education. The second is to identify the educational practices that will cultivate this kind of maturity and develop the institutional capacities and curricular designs that will implement these practices. These are adaptive changes and will reorder how a theological school will do its work.

Conclusion

Mainline Protestant schools invented institutional structures and educational strategies that have lasted for 150 years and that provided significant ballast in a time of substantive change. That ballast, however, will not be sufficient to carry these schools into the future. The structures these schools developed had educational coherence, denominational clarity, and disciplinary structure. The same structures and practices, however, will not have the same effect in the future as they had in the past.

What will make these schools as good in the future as they have been in the past? What is the trajectory of hope that will fit them for the future? There are several factors. The deep commitment they have evidenced to communities of color is a crucial asset for the future as well as the present. The future of these schools will be shaped by their ability to reinvent themselves, their capacity to sustain and renew religious commitments, their critical attentiveness to church and society, and the integrity of their intellectual practices. For many, the fiscal assets they have accrued—in facilities, property, and endowments—will provide necessary funds for the future shapes and practices they will adopt.

The future will neither recapture former cultural privilege or denominational capacity nor be a linear extension of the decline of the past decades. The mainline schools that were the first theological schools in the United States are not finished. The missions that have sustained these schools will continue. They will educate religious leaders, curate ancient wisdom, and engage new intellectual models. While denominational structures will change, communities of believers will continue to look to Christianity's sacred accrual for guidance in their lives and culture. These schools will serve as repositories for this accrual and incubators for new ways of understanding the Christian project in eras yet to come. While the social location of religion will change, the relevance of the Christian project will be undiminished. The future is hopeful, not because it will restore the past but because it will reconstruct theological education so that it will be as effective in a new day as it was for a day now gone.

Bibliography

Carroll, Jackson W., et al. *Being There: Culture and Formation in Two Theological Schools.* New York: Oxford University Press, 1997.

Farley, Edward. *Theologia: The Fragmentation and Unity of Theological Education.* Philadelphia: Fortress, 1983.

Foster, Charles, et al. *Educating Clergy: Teaching Practices and Pastoral Imagination.* San Francisco: Jossey-Bass, 2006.

Heifetz, Ronald. *Leadership without Easy Answers.* Cambridge, MA: Belknap Press of Harvard University Press, 1994.

Miller, Glenn. *Piety and Profession: American Protestant Theological Education, 1870-1970.* Grand Rapids: Eerdmans, 2007.

Padgett, John B. "Requiem for a Nun: Resources." *William Faulkner on the Web*, edited by John B. Padgett (July 2009). http://www.mcsr.olemiss.edu/~egjbp/faulkner/r_n_rfan.html#past.

2

America's Changing Religious and Cultural Landscape and Its Implications for Theological Education[1]

Nancy T. Ammerman

IN THE EARLY 1960S, few religious leaders probably realized quite what a turning point had been reached in American culture. At that point the postwar glow of growth was still intact, with the baby boom just winding down. Church attendance was still at all-time highs, and the system of denominational organization that had been established a half-century before was reaching full maturity. Catholics were emerging into the mainstream of American culture, and each religious group thought it could count on a well-established organizational and cultural clergy pipeline from youth group to denominational college to seminary and back to the pulpit, perhaps even with a detour for some time in a post-college denominational mission posting. Whether things ever worked quite this smoothly is hard to reconstruct at this distance, but there is little doubt that at its founding ATS entered a more predictable organizational and cultural world than the setting in which we do our work today (Roof and McKinney 1987).

---

1. Originally published in *Theological Education* 49.1 (2014) 27–34.

Changing Religious and Cultural Landscape

There are many changes on which we could focus—financial challenges and declining enrollments in many schools, the changing demographics and financial challenges of students themselves, or the erosion of connections between denominations and their seminaries—but I want to focus this brief essay around two kinds of issues. First I will explore the changes in American culture that have made the very notion of religious communities and religious leadership an increasing challenge. Why does it seem so hard to gather and sustain a congregation these days? Second, I will argue that in spite of the difficulties, religious communities are essential, not to be discarded as irrelevant. I will close with some reflections on meeting the leadership and educational challenges of gathering those communities.

One of the most startling changes in the last two decades has been the "rise of the nones," as Pew titled their report on the growing number of religiously unaffiliated people (Religion and Public Life 2012). One in five adult Americans now responds "none" to the question of religious identification, and among young adults, that number is one in three. As recently as the early 1990s, the number of adult nonaffiliates was under 10 percent, so this does represent a significant and rapid rise. Those who have long and eagerly awaited the decline of religion in "exceptional" America have celebrated with I-told-you-so fervor, while religious leaders have tended to console themselves with the reality that few of the nonaffiliates are hardcore atheists. People in the churches, in fact, often cite the rising chorus of talk about spirituality as a call to abandon declining institutions and join the seekers in pursuit of inner wisdom (Butler Bass 2013; Marler and Hadaway 2002). Perhaps the nones are not religious for good reason, and we should join them in seeking spirituality.

It is a bit difficult, however, to discern just what to make of that "spiritual but not religious" talk that seems so pervasive. Whatever it means, the people in that category are not the same as the "nones." Only about a third of the spiritual but not religious are unaffiliated; half attend worship with at least some regularity, two-thirds say religion is at least somewhat important to them, 70 percent pray at least occasionally, and nearly all of them believe in God. There is even a conservative evangelical version of this based on the notion that what matters is one's relationship with Jesus, not one's membership in a religion. The vast majority of the people who say they are spiritual, also say they are religious, and even the ones who say they aren't, are likely to look religious by most conventional measures.

Are the unaffiliated, then, spiritual seekers? Actually, no. Pew describes them as "nothing in particulars." They are no more likely to believe in "alternative" spiritualities than are Christians and other affiliates, and when asked if they are looking for a religious or spiritual connection, they say no. If religious leaders expect this population to wander back to church someday, that is probably not a good bet. Nor is it a good bet to think that they have deep spiritual insight that is the future of the faith. Based on these surveys and on my own research, if I had to describe the people who claim to be spiritual, but do not want to be called religious, I would say that they are open to the transcendent dimension in life and fairly sure that we aren't alone in the universe, but they have very little in their lives that actively connects them with a language for describing that or with practices that encourage it (Ammerman 2013). They are lurking around the edges of religious traditions—often for political reasons as much as for religious ones. They have few experiences of their own to discredit what they see in the news, and if that is what religion is, they want no part of it.

How did they get so disconnected? What church leaders in the 1960s had not quite seen yet is just what a transition we were entering. The "question authority" generation may have finally settled down and occasionally brought their children to church, but many of those children (today's young adults) never got the sustained religious education, tied to a single set of parents and siblings, that had characterized the earlier religious boom. Many of the social and cultural anchors that had historically sustained parish life began to shift in the 1960s (Wuthnow 2007; Fischer 1991; Douglass and Brunner 1935; Warner and Wittner 1998).

Changing Religious and Cultural Landscape

While residential mobility has happened at a roughly steady rate since World War II, recent declines in home ownership and recent decreases in job stability have combined to make shifting memberships an even more constant fact of life for congregations. For young adults, the rates of mobility are much higher, with one in six moving across county or state lines in each five year period. With job markets and career paths far more unpredictable and relationships far less settled, young adults have fewer commitments to keep them in one place and fewer well-worn paths leading toward a congregation.

For all mobile urban dwellers, the nature of "community" is much less tied to geography than it was even for the suburban residents of the 1950s and 1960s. The people who constitute a network of emotional support and everyday connection may be constituted around common interests and shared experiences more than blood and land. "Community" is something to be constructed rather than inherited, and that applies to congregations, as well. People who live in cities have as many family and friendship ties and help each other out in similar ways to rural dwellers—but their ties are not geography-based. And they may be maintained as much through phone and text and Facebook as through face-to-face contact. In part, young adults are disconnected from congregations in much the same way they are disconnected from other institutions and potentially connected to congregations to the extent that new forms of connection become part of congregational life.

One of the other significant shifts in the American cultural landscape was also just on the horizon in the early 1960s, namely immigration reform. The 1965 immigration law radically increased the flow of immigrants and dramatically changed their cultures of origin. By the end of the century, the US was home to as big a proportion of immigrants as it had been a century earlier, but rather than coming almost entirely from Europe, our new immigrant population began to bring a broader array of ethnic and religious diversity into our midst. We have become visibly aware that we are not just a Christian and Jewish country. At least as important, however, are the effects within Christianity itself.

These new migrant flows have largely been from countries where Christianity is the dominant religion, and in other countries, it is Christians who are disproportionately present among the emigrants. So, while it is true that we are increasingly multi-religious, it is also true that the larger trend is what Warner calls "the de-Europeanization of American Christianity"(Warner 2005; Aging 2010). Some of the fastest growing segments of American religion are Korean Methodists and Presbyterians, Salvadoran Pentecostals, and Mexican Catholics.

Both in seminary classrooms and in the communities graduates will serve, the image of a Euro-American male pastor serving a stable community of ethnically similar, two-parent families is now radically out of sync with reality. In addition to the changing ethnic and religious composition of American communities, the very shape of family life has changed, as well. At the end of the 1950s, half of all American households consisted of parents with young children; today that proportion is one in five. While the number of nonaffiliated people has risen in most demographic groups, straight married people with children, even those in the youngest cohorts, are almost as likely to be affiliated today as they were in the 1960s—there just aren't nearly as many such families out there. There are more blended families, of course, and families with same-sex parents, but most of all, there are more people living alone and more living as couples both before and after children. In fact, the fastest-growing segment of the population is those over eighty. Retired people today can expect to live for two decades, and neither the culture, the healthcare system, nor the churches are really ready for that reality.

All of these changes have wreaked havoc on the ways people thought about forming communities and on the expectation that a congregation would be a central part of that community. As people have moved from place to place and job to job and relationship to relationship, the task of creating networks of support and mutual responsibility has become increasingly challenging. All of these changes have sent an increasingly disparate assortment of students to theological schools—young and old, shaped in congregations themselves and not, representing the increasingly diverse range of families, cultures, and theologies that make up American communities. When they think about the communities they have come from and the communities they will lead, there are many models in their heads.

But in spite of the challenges, the things that happen in local congregations are more important than ever—to the individuals in them, to the larger society in which we all live, and to the faith traditions theological educators participate in.

Even the "nones" agree that congregations and other faith-based organizations are important to the well-being of our society. Congregations are often the only spaces in which otherwise marginalized populations can celebrate their own cultures and organize their own public life. They are also critical players in the increasingly frayed safety net that protects the most vulnerable. They not only provide services, but also mobilize advocacy and model what it means to take care of each other and the common good. People who participate give more, vote more, and volunteer more (Putnam and Campbell 2010). The work congregations do even extends to mobilizing the energies of people who merely have friends who participate. When congregations are not present and healthy, there is a big hole in the overall social fabric.

Churches and synagogues are not just good voluntary community organizations, of course, modeling and passing along traditions of virtue that are critical to our larger culture. They are also the places where people are invited into an experience of transcendence and a relationship with the divine. If we care about the presence of faith in the world, the work of theological education must continue to include attention to the formation and leadership of collective religious gatherings, whatever form they may take. My own recent research on spirituality in everyday life has convinced me yet again that congregating matters. A life story that has spiritual content and direction is much more likely to come from someone who is an active participant in a religious community. For all the talk about people being "spiritual but not religious" and all the lore about finding God in the woods, I can tell you that there are very, very few people out there who are truly pursuing a spiritual way of life without the help of a religious community of some sort.

People who carry their faith into the world are people who experience and practice the presence of faith in shared work and shared conversations. When communities gather around ritual and learning and common labor, they provide the arenas in which spiritual conversation and spiritual relationships happen. Those who are only moderately involved in organized participation get some of this benefit, but it is the active participant (no matter what tradition) who occupies the fertile conversational spaces of religious communities. While preaching and music and education for their children are the threshold experiences that keep many people coming at a fairly regular pace, it is participation in smaller-group activities that provides the space for making the deeper connections—to other people and by way of the conversations with those people, between faith and life. Those who are on the margins of religious life, on the other hand, still somewhat connected but inactive, are more likely alienated because a congregation has failed in its relational work than because they have ceased to believe. Connections and conversations are the building blocks of the new kinds of religious communities our best students will learn to lead.

Today's culture makes it exceedingly difficult to get people in the door of any religious organization, and the unsettledness of all our connections is hard soil in which to grow any sort of community. Being a religious leader no longer means stepping into a ready-made community; it means building one. Simply teaching the basic skills of preaching and teaching will not help students assemble the disparate pilgrims moving through the city to hear what they have to say. Simply ensuring adequate scriptural and theological knowledge may or may not help a student hear the halting questions of a young adult who has never been to church. Simply providing an accredited religious credential will not matter if the people who need to be gathered into a community have never heard of your denomination (let alone the Association of Theological Schools). All the things seminaries have learned to do are still essential, but they are no longer sufficient. Today's religious leaders have to invite people into a spiritual community where worship introduces connections to God, fellowship introduces connections to each other, and service introduces connections to a larger mission in the world.

In today's religious and cultural landscape, the people who leave our theological schools cannot assume that the spiritual community will already be there or that it will be healthy and intact. Both repair and new construction may be needed. As soon as a group has been built, it will have to adjust to the constant flux of new people and new challenges. Blessing people who leave will be as much a part of the task as welcoming new people who arrive. Networking by all means possible will be as much a part of a leader's toolkit as the mimeograph machine of old. Although it may be much more difficult to gather a community, it is more critical than ever. The work of theological education is no less necessary—just different.

Bibliography

Administration on Aging. *A Profile of Older Americans: 2010*. Department of Health & Human Services 2010. http://www.aoa.gov/aoaroot/aging_statistics/Profile/2010/16.aspx, 2012.

Ammerman, Nancy Tatom. *Sacred Stories, Spiritual Tribes: Finding Religion in Everyday Life*. New York: Oxford University Press, 2013.

Butler Bass, Diana. *Christianity After Religion: The End of Church and the Birth of a New Spiritual Awakening*. New York: HarperOne, 2013.

Douglass, H. Paul, and Edmund de S. Brunner. *The Protestant Church as a Social Institution*. New York: Harper and Row, 1935.

Fischer, Claude S. "Ambivalent Communities: How Americans understand their localities." In *America at Century's End*, edited by A. Wolfe, 79–91. Berkeley, CA: University of California Press, 1991.

Marler, Penny Long, and C. Kirk Hadaway. "'Being Religious' or 'Being Spiritual' in America: A Zero-Sum Proposition?" *Journal for the Scientific Study of Religion* 41, no. 2 (2002) 289–300.

Pew Forum on Religion and Public Life. "Nones" on the Rise: One-in-Five Adults Have No Religious Affiliation. http://www.pewforum.org/files/2012/10/NonesOnTheRise-full.pdf, 2012.

Putnam, Robert D., and David E. Campbell. *American Grace: How Religion Divides and Unites Us*. New York: Simon & Schuster, 2010.

Roof, Wade Clark, and William McKinney. *American Mainline Religion*. New Brunswick, NJ: Rutgers University Press, 1987.

Warner, R. Stephen. "The De-Europeanization of American Christianity." In *A Church of Our Own: Disestablishment and Diversity in American Religion*, edited by R. S. Warner, 257–62. New Brunswick, NJ: Rutgers University Press, 2005.

Warner, R. Stephen, and Judith G. Wittner, eds. *Gatherings in Diaspora: Religious Communities and the New Immigration*. Philadelphia: Temple University Press, 1998.

Wuthnow, Robert. *After the Baby Boomers: How Twenty- and Thirty-Somethings are Shaping the Future of American Religion*. Princeton, NJ: Princeton University Press, 2007.

3

Embracing a Greater, Higher Calling
Redefining the Mission and Purpose of the Freestanding Protestant Seminary

BENJAMÍN VALENTÍN

THOSE WHO WORK IN or are affiliated with freestanding mainline Protestant theological schools are well aware of the challenges these schools face today. They might even say they are too well aware of them. After all, the challenges are often mentioned in faculty meetings; in trustees' board meetings; in administrative meetings; and in the chance conversations that spring up among colleagues during day-to-day interaction in the hallways, cafeterias, and copy rooms. They are even being talked about now with greater frequency in journals and periodicals that focus on topics and issues in higher education or theological education (e.g. *The Chronicle of Higher Education, Theological Education, In Trust,* and *Auburn Studies*). And besides the conversations and written reports, there are of course the visible signs that reveal struggle and in many cases decline: fewer students in the classrooms; fewer new student applications; the weathered buildings that make evident the symptoms of deferred maintenance due to declining income; and the recurrent selling of buildings, library holdings, libraries, land, and other assets to offset diminishing revenue. These traits tell a story.

Indeed, if one works in or is affiliated with a freestanding mainline Protestant seminary, there is a good chance not only that one will be acquainted with this prevalent story of struggle and decline but also with the story behind the story. There is a good chance, in other words, that one will be privy to the stated reasons for these struggles. The controlling influence of secularism and its negative effect on religious institutions; the growing social disinterest in organized religion; the decline of mainline Protestant denominations; the declining attractiveness of ecclesiastical leadership as a career choice among young people; the increasing disinterest in certain types of public service-oriented or lower-salaried professions; the corresponding drop off in seminary student enrollment; the enduring effect of the 2008 economic recession; the predictable decline in financial contributions from friends, alums, church denominations, foundations, and other traditional supporters of the enterprise of theological education; the institutional liabilities that come with the small-scale and unallied, independent status of these schools; the wearing effect over time of bad organization, inadequate management, unwise investment of endowment funds, and a prevailing inability to raise funds in a changing religious climate; these are some of the recognized challenges freestanding Protestant seminaries face today.

It should be clear that many of these are not self-imposed or internally caused problems. What I mean is that seminaries cannot be blamed for the rise of some of these difficulties, not directly at least. Seminaries are not entirely responsible, if at all, for the emergence of secularization, the decline of the mainline Protestant denominations, or the growing social disinterest in organized religion, for instance. Perhaps they can be faulted for slowness in recognizing and responding to these social and ecclesiastical realities, but not for their creation. Similarly, seminaries cannot be blamed for economic downturns or for changes in career preferences within our society. These can be seen as broader social and ecclesiastical circumstances that transcend the control of seminaries. One could say that this is simply the hand seminaries have been dealt in our late modern era, and it is up to them to learn how to play the hand they're dealt. On the other hand, we must admit that some of the problems mentioned above can be attributed to the mind-set, choices, actions, and inabilities of the seminaries themselves. Seminaries can be blamed for succumbing to bad organizational and administrative tendencies; for mishandling endowment funds; for being inattentive to the long-term costs and risks of deferred building maintenance; and for their inability to find ways to raise funds, among other things. And there is no doubt that these kinds of mishaps have compromised the welfare of many seminaries.

But there is another long-standing, ingrained tendency that has impaired the prosperity or good fortune of seminaries, and it is one that is often overlooked, perhaps because it is so deep-rooted as to be assumed. I am referring to the instinctive assumption that the ultimate, if not sole, purpose of theological education is to train people for ordained or professional ministry, and specifically for pastoral ministry in a congregation. This presupposition is so long-established and fixed that if they were to be asked to define what a seminary is, most seminary administrators and professors, and indeed even those people in the general public who have ever heard of such a school, would probably say that a seminary is a preparatory school for congregational ministry. What this shows is that the vocation of the seminary, and the nature and mission of the theological education these schools offer, has come to be defined by the prospect, aims, and pursuit of one profession—the profession of pastoral ministry.

As we will see, this mind-set is understandable given the historical origins of seminaries as schools of and for the church. And there may have been a time, many decades ago, when freestanding Protestant seminaries could get by with such a narrow focus and sense of purpose. But that was then and this is now. In other words, times and circumstances have changed. And seminaries must be willing to adapt to changes that have occurred in the churches and in our society if they are to survive and thrive. Specifically, they will need to adopt a wider, deeper, grander understanding of the task of theology and the mission of a seminary. To put it in "churchy" terms, I believe that seminaries need to seek, make room for, and embrace a greater (dare I say higher?) calling—a calling that includes not only the pursuit of and preparation for ministry but also the fostering of other "professions" and pursuits aimed at the search for transcendence and the building of a more sacred, compassionate, just, and peaceful world. In the pages that follow I will try to explain why I am making this proposal, while also trying to throw light upon some paths that seminaries could pursue in their attempt to live into this grander calling.

In a Niche within a Niche— Not Always a Good Place to Be

We begin by exploring at greater length the penchant I bemoan. In this regard, I will say that the mentality I am worrying about typically expresses itself through the belief that seminaries exist to prepare ministers for the church. To be sure, I want to clarify that seminaries often do allow for the possibility that students may come to them for other reasons, and with other forms of learning and vocations in mind, besides those that are often associated with the pursuit of a career in congregational ministry. They try, therefore, to offer courses and programs that could be of use to persons pursuing other walks of life. I am not adverting to a zero-sum scenario then when I express distress over a kind of vocational and missional myopia that is stifling the success of many freestanding Protestant seminaries. Nevertheless, it is undeniable that seminaries do not always shine in the area of emphasizing the possibility of other career paths besides the one of ordained clergyperson. They may recognize, accommodate, and harbor these possible "others" or "other professions" in their programming, but rarely do our schools give prominence to them or treat them with the same regard as pastoral ministry.

Pastoral ministry is usually regarded as the holy grail of a seminary education, and the perspective and attitude our schools tend to project is that seminaries are in the business of preparing ministers for the church. That this is their true mission and purpose is mostly assumed. So it is hardly surprising that this outlook turns up in much of what our seminaries say and do.

It emerges, for instance, in the advertising and marketing plans our schools devise; in the inadvertent messages our school officers frequently convey during open house events and new student orientation programs; in the teaching methods our schools often employ; in the workshops and lecture series our schools tend to promote; and in the hiring and fundraising practices our schools commonly embrace. It even comes into view in and generally guides our new student recruiting practices in terms of where we will look for new recruits (i.e., mostly in the churches) and in terms of who we will try the hardest to recruit (i.e., students who aspire to ministry in and for the church). In short, the outlook to which I am referring is pretty influential and conspicuous even if at times inadvertent or involuntary, given its character and functioning as a form of assumption or ingrained "habit of the heart." And the message it tends to convey to those within the seminaries and those outside of them is this: a seminary is a place you come to if you want to prepare for, and if you want to help people prepare for, a career in congregational ministry.

The prevalence of this particular understanding of a seminary's mission and purpose is understandable in the light of the history of American Protestant theological education. If one examines the origin of the first American Protestant seminaries in the early nineteenth century, one will find that they were established with two purposes in mind. First, they were founded by American Protestant leaders to create "safe" institutional spaces in which prospective ministers could become proficient in the acknowledged teachings of the different Protestant ecclesial traditions while remaining at a distance from the "enlightened" or Enlightenment-based skepticism, secularism, and liberalism that was on the rise in the broader world of learning. Second, seminaries were founded by these leaders to ensure that prospective young clerics would be a) educated in a highly technical and precise type of theological thought; b) prepared for their future duties in the church; c) equipped to transmit the acknowledged teachings of the particular Protestant ecclesial bodies to present and future generations of Christian converts; and d) fitted to make a contribution to the goal of an American Christian civilization.[1]

These goals may contain some differentiation within them, but it should be evident that they each converge at and point to the church or churches. Those who founded seminaries determined to establish new institutions that could preserve the different ecclesial or denominational traditions and promote the professional training of ministers for the different churches or denominations (e.g., the Reformed, Lutheran, Anglican, Presbyterian, Congregationalist, Methodist, and Baptist ecclesial bodies). As a matter of fact, these objectives flowed into one another inasmuch as the hope was that denominational traditions could be preserved through the professional training of ministers. It could be said that from the start the schools we know of as seminaries were deeply rooted in confessionalism and clericalism. In other words, these have been schools of and for the churches from the outset. It is not surprising, then, that the understanding of a seminary as a place where one goes to train for congregational ministry in a particular denomination has remained in place through the years, seeing that this understanding of a seminary's mission and purpose was implanted into the mind-set of these schools from the very beginning. And, in one sense, one could say that there is nothing wrong with this institutional sense of mission and purpose. The vocation of congregational ministry is a noble one, of course, and the goal of preparing learned ministers for the churches is equally honorable and important.

But it is important to note that this rather specialized and, I would say, restricted sense of mission and purpose hasn't exactly served freestanding mainline Protestant seminaries well across the years. Not in the areas of student recruitment and enrollment, institutional growth, and financial stability at least. If one examines the history of the great majority of freestanding

---

1. For more on the aims and purposes of the first American Protestant seminary founders, see Miller, *Piety and Intellect*, esp. 1–37.

mainline Protestant seminaries, one will discover a common story of incessant struggle. Most of these schools have remained small, minutely endowed, and under-utilized, and they have usually had to struggle for their very existence all through the years. It is true that from 1820 to 1970 American Protestants rapidly established a significant number of new theological seminaries.[2] But, as Glen Miller, the great historian of American Protestant theological education, has noted, "one could wonder why people thought that new schools should be built"[3] even while older ones were often struggling for their existence. Freestanding American Protestant seminaries were not exactly thriving in those first 150 years or so of seminary founding. It is more correct to say that they were able to get by thanks to their narrow focus on ministerial learning. But they were able to manage this modest achievement only because the mainline Protestant churches were still thriving in the nineteenth and early twentieth centuries. That is no longer the case, and seminaries have been grieving this change in the life of the church. Even if seminaries managed to make do with their heavy focus on parish ministry when the mainline Protestant churches were doing well, it is at the very least debatable whether they can continue to do so now that these churches have fallen on hard times.

The decline of the mainline Protestant denominations in the United States is one of the better-known religious trends of our time. Many studies have examined this decades-long trend, including some major ones, such as the General Social Survey (GSS), the National Congregations Study (NCS), the Pew Forum on America's Changing Religious Landscape conducted by the Pew Research Center, and the National Survey of Mainline Protestant Churches conducted by the Barna Group. Research and polling carried out by the *Yearbook of American & Canadian Churches*, the Auburn Center for the Study of Theological Education, and the

---

2. For more on the topic of the rapid establishment of seminaries, especially early on in the nineteenth century and through the middle of the twentieth century, see Miller's *Piety and Intellect* and *Piety and Profession*.

3. Miller, *Piety and Intellect*, 5.

Association of Theological Schools also speaks to the protracted phenomenon. And there are, of course, the countless news reports that say something on the topic.[4] It has received much scrutiny from many different data and news service sources, therefore, and what they all invariably relate is a prevailing story of significant and sustained decline.

Half a century ago, the seven Protestant denominations that are generally included under the "mainline" umbrella were still enjoying appreciable prosperity. I do think that it is wise to question the somewhat exaggerated accounts that relate a tale of mainline Protestant domination in the American religious landscape of the nineteenth and early-to-mid twentieth century. It is likely, after all, that the mainline Protestant groups never represented anything close to a majority of US Americans and that they never really were the authoritative center of American religion in the way some have suggested.[5] But one can at least speak in terms of "appreciable prosperity" with regard to the standing of these particular church bodies in nineteenth- and early-to-mid twentieth-century America. The mainline or old-line denominations to which I have been referring—i.e., The United Methodist Church; the Evangelical Lutheran Church in America (ELCA); the Presbyterian Church (USA); the Episcopal Church; the American Baptist Churches in the USA; the United Church of Christ (UCC); and the Christian Church (Disciples of Christ)—grew steadily every year since the early years of our nation or since their establishment until the mid-1960s, increasing in the number of their respective churches and members. The fortune and fortunes of this cohort of Protestant churches started to change sometime around 1965, however.

Figures offered by studies and surveys indicate that the growth of these denominations slowed down in the early 1960s, and that after the middle of the decade they had begun to lose members and churches. It is estimated, for instance, that the number of mainline churches dropped from more than 80,000 in the 1950s

---

4. Another great source for studying the decline of mainline Protestant denominations is Chaves, *American Religion*, esp. 81–93.

5. For more on this topic and likelihood, see Campbell, "Glory Days?"

to about 72,000 in 2009.⁶ The downtrend is even more glaring when one considers mainline church membership and the share of Americans who affiliate with a mainline church. Official church membership figures provided by the mainline denominations reveal that the combined membership of these denominations in the early 1950s was somewhere in the neighborhood of 40 million members or active attendees. In 1965 the figure was 31 million. From 1965 to 1988, mainline church membership declined from 31 million to 25 million. In 2005 the figure stood at 21 million, with some estimates suggesting a number of roughly 20 million people by 2009.⁷ If these numbers are correct, we are talking about a startling membership decline of nearly 50 percent in six decades. And as for the matter of the general percentage of Americans affiliated with a mainline denomination, it is noteworthy that while in 1970 the mainline churches could claim 30 percent of the US population as members today they can only claim about 14 percent of all Americans in the USA.⁸

These figures vary to some extent depending on the source or study one consults. But what does not change is the consistent reporting of a noticeable decline in the numbers of churches and members, and in the percentage of Americans affiliated with the mainline denominations. No matter the source, the recounting of some sort of decline remains the same. The best that the positive reports can do is to inform us that in more recent years the descent has slowed a bit.⁹ These are not exactly bullish or inspiring reports, in other words. Noteworthy too is the fact that there are several signs that point to this being a long-term downward trend that is not likely to be reversed any time soon. For instance, it has been reported that since 1999 there has been a 22 percent drop in the

---

6. See the Barna Group Report, *The State of Mainline Protestant Churches* (December 7, 2009).

7. For these and other figures on mainline church membership, see Linder, ed., *Yearbook of American and Canadian Churches*; and Hout et al., "The Demographic Imperative in Religious Change in the United States."

8. For this last statistic see Chaves, *American Religion*, 87.

9. See, for instance, Gryboski, "The Decline of Decline?" *The Christian Post* (October 20, 2014).

percentage of adults attending mainline congregations who have children under the age of eighteen living in their home. A related statistic shows that while young adults of twenty-five years of age or younger make up 6 percent of the national population, they constitute only 2 percent of all adults attending mainline churches.[10] This does not bode well for the potential future membership of these churches and denominations. And another present and future challenge for the mainline ecclesiastical bodies is their inability to attract ethnic minorities, especially Latino/as and Asians. It so happens that these are social groups that have grown in numbers within the United States. But the mainline denominations and churches have struggled in reaching them. Latino/as make up 16 percent of the US population but only 6 percent of the mainline population. "Asians represent 4% of the American public, but only half that population among mainline congregants."[11] These statistics and facts lead one to believe that the mainline churches may be on the cusp of a long-term decline. One will certainly encounter individual churches that have managed to avert this downward trend. However, the broad picture portrays a group of churches that has lost ground in the last several decades with respect to its membership count, number of congregations, and share of the US population. Moreover, the downward trend looks to be a lengthy one and it is difficult to see how it might be reversed anytime soon.

This picture should trouble the mainline Protestant denominational bodies, leading them to pore over the possible reasons for their decline and to explore potential correctives in response to it. But the picture draws in the mainline Protestant seminaries as well. The struggles of the mainline Protestant denominations have reached the grounds and corridors of these schools, compromising their standing, especially in the areas of fundraising and student enrollment. Report after report put forth in the last decade either by the Auburn Center for the Study of Theological Education, *In Trust*, or the Association of Theological Schools, tells of the worsening situation of the mainline denominational seminaries in

---

10. For both of these figures, see The Barna Group Report, *The State of Mainline Protestant Churches*.

11. The Barna Group Report, *The State of Mainline Protestant Churches*.

these important areas. When reading these reports, one discovers that seminaries reporting to the Association of Theological Schools have experienced a 24.3 percent decline in financial support from all church sources since 2006, going from a collective figure of $154 million contributed from church sources in FY 2006 to one of $117 million in 2011.[12] We discover too that this trend of decline in church support for theological education has been going on for some time in the mainline Protestant seminaries. These schools reported diminishing church funding from 1991–2001.[13]

As for enrollment trends, reports disclose a shrinking seminary population. Seminaries have never been large schools to begin with, of course. In 2012 the Association of Theological Schools (ATS) reported a total headcount of 74,223 students in 268 schools. The figure was 69,101 for the 230 US-based seminaries.[14] That total headcount figure should give one an idea of the small scale of the schools in question. To put that figure in perspective, some individual state universities have as many or more students than all of the schools that are currently members of the ATS combined.[15] When it comes to seminaries, we are talking about schools that often count on having 250–350 students, with the largest school having about 3,500 students and some schools having even less than the median enrollment at an ATS school, which is 155 students.[16] These are very small schools, in other words.

So when we speak of a decline in seminary enrollment we need to keep in mind that we are not talking about a monumental number of students. But, precisely because of their minute size, one could say that numbers matter even more to the schools we call seminaries. Every single student is important in their case, and any decrease in the number of enrolled students carries increased significance in the matter of the footing, outlook, and viability of

12. See Ruger and Meinzer, "Through Trial and Tribulation," 16.

13. Ruger and Meinzer, "Through Trial and Tribulation," 14–15.

14. These figures derive from the ATS website. See www.ats.edu/resources/institutional-data/annual-data-tables.

15. Consider, for instance, that Arizona State University has 73,373 students in its multicampus system.

16. See Henson and Hoag, "More Schools, Fewer Students," 16.

these theological schools. To put it simply, because they are already small, seminaries cannot afford a shrinking population. This is especially so because most of them rely heavily on student tuition payments for their finances. Barbara Wheeler and Anthony Ruger are absolutely right when they say that "a shrinking population is the most corrosive problem" a seminary can face.[17] "It inflicts financial damage on campuses that rely primarily on tuition payments, and even schools with generous endowments find that undersized courses dampen the morale of faculty, staff, and students." "Most troubling," Wheeler and Ruger go on to say, "a dearth of students raises fundamental questions: Is the mission of the school still relevant? Is it needed in its present form?"[18]

For these reasons, those who work in or are affiliated with seminaries should be very alarmed by the recent reports that reveal that all schools that are currently members of the Association of Theological Schools show enrollment trending downward.[19] It is estimated that the median ATS seminary has lost about 8 percent of its enrollment since 2001.[20] This is an aggregate figure, however. In other words, it lumps together all the different types of theological schools including evangelical schools, non-denominational schools, Roman Catholic schools, Protestant schools, and even university-based divinity schools, among others. Some of these have not been as affected by the downward direction of enrollment trends (e.g. the university-based divinity schools, non-denominational schools, and the Roman Catholic schools), and this spruces up the numbers somewhat and helps to mask the decline being experienced at other types of schools. But the rate of enrollment decline at the mainline Protestant seminaries is known to be

---

17. See Wheeler and Ruger, "Sobering Figures Point to Overall Enrollment Decline," 5.

18. Wheeler and Ruger, "Sobering Figures Point to Overall Enrollment Decline," 5.

19. Wheeler and Ruger, "Sobering Figures Point to Overall Enrollment Decline," 9.

20. See Henson and Hoag, "More Schools, Fewer Students," 16.

higher.[21] In some cases the fall-off can be pronounced. My former school (Andover Newton Theological School), for instance, saw its headcount decrease by 39 percent and its full-time equivalency by 28 percent between the 2000–2001 and the 2015–2016 academic years. But most other freestanding mainline denominational seminaries are in the same boat, seeing their enrollment numbers decline steadily year after year on the one hand and their finances dwindle precipitously on the other, on account of the fall-off in student numbers and the drop-off in church support for theological education. It is enough, or should be enough, I presume, to make these schools start to ask some deep questions about their relevance in a changing social, religious, and ecclesial context and about their future viability in their current form.

Trying situations, be they in life or in the case of institutions or an industry even, tend to be caused by multiple factors or occurrences. Likewise, their remedy or mitigation usually requires deliberation and well-advised effort on various fronts rather than a single one. The same can be said about the "existential" crisis most seminaries, and especially the freestanding mainline Protestant seminaries, are facing today. It can be attributed to various root causes, and will surely require creative initiative and action in multiple realms. But I am convinced that a major reason why most seminaries, and especially the freestanding mainline Protestant seminaries, are struggling for their existence is because they have yielded to and have been constrained by a narrow sense of mission and purpose. Because they have mostly confined their sense of educational mission and purpose to the goal of preparing ministers for the churches, and because this is the sense of mission and purpose they generally convey to the outside world, these schools have ended up tying their lot to a rapidly shrinking audience, client base, and, dare we say, "market."

The relation between the struggles of the mainline Protestant seminaries and the travails of the mainline Protestant denominations should be easy to see, I believe. As the number of churches declines and as the size of many of the remaining mainline

---

21. See Wheeler et al., "Theological Student Enrollment."

churches shrinks, there is quite naturally less of a need or demand for church ministers in these mainline bodies. Moreover, the numerical decline in the mainline Protestant churches translates to a smaller pool of candidates for seminary education to begin with. Add to this the fact that religious leadership is a less attractive career choice for young people than it used to be, and the fact that more than one-third of those now serving in ministry and almost one-half of those in other occupations say they would recommend ministry "only with reservations," and you have yourself a challenging, unfavorable, and even calamitous situation if you are solely or primarily in the business of educating ministers for parish ministry.[22] It is little wonder why most seminaries today are struggling to stay open; why some have had to close; and why others have had to go the route of becoming "embedded schools" in larger educational institutions, which essentially means that they have had to sell off their campuses and properties, dismiss most of their personnel, and relinquish much of their autonomy in order to become smaller entities within a larger acquiring educational institution. The challenge is that of remaining alive or "in business" when there is less need or desire for the educational product you have to offer.

But, again, my point and/or contention here is that seminaries have largely created and placed themselves in this dire situation by limiting the mission and purpose of theological education to the goal of training people for parish ministry. Essentially, seminaries have succeeded in creating what I like to call "a niche within a niche." In this case, we are talking about a superniche market, or if you'd prefer, a superniche educational enterprise that appeals to and is germane to fewer and fewer people in our day and age. The study of the conceivability of a transcendent being or realm; of the possibility of human transcendence; of the wonder and bewilderment of the phenomenon of religion; of the influence of religion; and of the history, configurations, particularities, and continuing significance of our religious communities and traditions: these

---

22. For more on these trends, see Chaves's *American Religion*, esp. 69–80; and Wheeler et al., "How Are We Doing?," 16.

investigative undertakings would already constitute a niche venture with appeal to a select segment of the population. To compress this educational enterprise even further by aligning it almost exclusively with the aspirations and goal of one profession (i.e., parish ministry) is to create a "niche within a niche"—a niche within a niche venture—that appeals to, is relevant to, and contributes to a tiny, very limited, and increasingly shrinking public. This, basically, is what seminaries have done.

If seminaries are not only to survive but to thrive, and if seminaries are to appeal to a larger public and to play a bigger and more vital role in the process of building a more sacred, just, compassionate, and peaceful world, they will need to do a better job of conveying the message that a theological education provides a variety of resources, competencies, and learning that can be applied to different vocations, callings, and activities. But before this can transpire, a shift towards a broader, more expansive understanding of the mission and purpose of a seminary will need to occur in these schools.

We who work in seminaries or theological schools—we seminary presidents, executives, board members, administrators, and faculty members—should try more consistently to think of and speak of our seminaries as being more than just preacher/pastor factories. This customary viewing of the seminary has proven to be too limiting, too stifling over time, and especially in recent time. We need a broader view and understanding of a seminary's mission and purpose. And I think that we can find some inspiring, guiding examples outside of our industry for the kind of shift in thinking that is needed in ours. For example, I think that the success story of Starbucks Coffee Company has a thing or two to teach us about the important role a broader sense of mission can play in building a successful enterprise and institution. So, why not turn to it for a bit of—dare I say "cup of"—inspiration?

To Starbucks for a Cup of Inspiration

The Starbucks Coffee Company has received much attention in the last ten to fifteen years in the world of business and in the world of the study of institutional leadership, and this for its amazing story of growth, corporate reinvention, and fiscal success. It has been the subject of numerous magazine and newspaper articles, and of various books as well.[23] Even theologians and religious scholars have found inspiration in its success and popularity.[24]

And why not? After all, we are talking about a company that went from being a roaster and retailer of whole bean and ground coffee with a single store in Seattle's Pike Place Market in 1971 to an American global coffeehouse company and global brand with 23,571 stores in seventy countries today. We are also talking about a company that reported figures of $19.2 billion in total revenue; $2.76 billion in net income; and a global sales growth figure of 16.4 percent in 2015.[25] I will add that this is a company that keeps adding to its massive and impressive throng of loyal customers each day, and that opens up a new Starbucks store somewhere in the

---

23. For some examples of books written about Starbucks see, Sara Gilbert, *Built for Success: The Story of Starbucks* (Mankato, MA: Creative Paperbacks, 2011); Joseph A. Michelli, *The Starbucks Experience: 5 Principles for Turning Ordinary Into Extraordinary* (New York: McGraw-Hill, 2007) and *Leading the Starbucks Way: 5 Principles for Connecting with Your Customers, Your Products, and Your People* (New York: McGraw-Hill, 2014); Michael T. Moe, *Finding the Next Starbucks: How to Identify and Invest in the Hot Stocks of Tomorrow* (New York: Penguin, 2006); John Moore, *Tribal Knowledge: Business Wisdom Brewed From the Grounds of Starbucks* (Chicago: Kaplan, 2006); John Schultz and Dori Jones Yang, *Pour Your Heart Into It: How Starbucks Built a Company One Cup at a Time* (New York: Hachette, 1997); Howard Schultz, *Onward: How Starbucks Fought for Its Life without Losing Its Soul* (New York: Rodale, 2011); John Simmons, *My Sister's A Barista: How They Made Starbucks A Home Away From Home* (Great Britain: Cyan, 2005).

24. See, for instance, Paul Copan, *When God Goes to Starbucks: A Guide to Everyday Apologetics* (Grand Rapids: Baker, 2008); and Leonard Sweet, *The Gospel According to Starbucks: Living With a Grande Passion* (Colorado Springs: Waterbrook, 2007).

25. See "By the Numbers: 18 Interesting Starbucks Statistics (March 2016)" at http://expandedramblings.com; and Starbucks Corp Profile at www.marketwatch.com.

Embracing a Greater, Higher Calling

world every single business day. No matter the index used, one has to admit that Starbucks has been a highly successful company.

It is no wonder, then, that the success story of this company has been closely followed and studied. And various decisions, strategies, practices, and feats taken, pursued, and/or effectuated by Starbucks have frequently been highlighted in the attempt to explain the basis of its success: Its emphasis on product quality, and its consistent ability to sell the best possible fresh-roasted whole-bean coffee and to make one of the best cups of coffee in the business. Its stroke of genius of wanting to offer Americans "a third place" of sorts—(a comfortable, casual, multipurpose location between home and the work place)—where they can come to meet friends; take quiet moments to gather themselves and their thoughts; read a book or newspaper; surf the Internet; do some work on the side; or just pick up a food or beverage treat to enjoy before, during, or after a long day of work. Its savvy designing and decorating of stores to exude a friendly ambience, community spirit, and pleasing aesthetic. Its conveyance of a personal touch, by having their baristas write a person's name on a paper, plastic, or ceramic cup when his or her drink is being prepared, so that people can feel special, important, and cared for. Its successful use of the retail technique known as "clustering"—(i.e., the opening up of several shops in close proximity)—to saturate certain areas with its presence and achieve market dominance. Its ingenious forging of institutional partnerships with other successful companies like Pepsi, Dreyer's Grand Ice Cream, and Spotify to enhance the "Starbucks experience" in its stores or to reach out to far more potential customers than those who come into its stores with a variety of product offerings. Its ability to present itself to the wider public as a responsible company, as a great company that frequently tries to strike a balance between profitability and a social conscience. These factors have received much attention in the attempt to explain why Starbucks has been so successful in a relatively short time. And there is no doubt that all these factors have played an important part in this company's success. But the key to Starbucks' success, at the most basic or fundamental level of things, has been its ability to appeal to a broad range of target audiences. In other words, Starbucks has managed to appeal to a broad range of customers. It is important to note, however, that Starbucks' knack in the area of broad appeal required an expanded vision and sense of mission in relation to its "core business." And this is the point I want to accentuate here in relation to seminaries.

When Starbucks first opened in 1971, it saw itself as an establishment that was in the business of selling whole-bean and ground coffee in bags for home consumption. To help their customers in the process of grinding and brewing the coffee at home, Starbucks began selling coffee-making equipment soon after its opening. But apart from the occasional coffee samples brewed for customers to taste, there wasn't a coffee-drinking experience to be had in the original Starbucks store itself. The purpose of the shop was clear and simple: it was to sell whole-bean and ground coffee for customers to grind, brew, and drink at home.[26]

This was the extent of Starbucks' original business identity and business errand. And it did well enough within that niche to allow the business to grow into a small Seattle retailer with five stores by 1982. But expansion beyond Seattle was not on the agenda at this time, nor would it have been likely given the inevitable hardships of most small retailers and the narrow confines that the original business owners—Jerry Baldwin, Zeo Siegl, and Gordon Bowker—had set for themselves.

Things began to change in 1987, however. Purchased in 1987 by Howard Schultz, and under his executive leadership from that moment on, Starbucks began a process of expanding its understanding of its core business to a far wider concentric circle. First it decided to offer a coffee drinking experience in store, adding beverage sales to the bean and ground coffee sales. Then in 1994 it decided to move outside the four walls of its stores and, through partnerships with other food and beverage companies, to invent new ways to enjoy the flavor of coffee in bottled beverages, ice

---

26. For more on the original business philosophy of Starbucks see Howard Schultz's *Pour Your Heart Into It,* esp. 24–37, and John Simmons's *My Sister's A Barista,* esp. 20–39.

Embracing a Greater, Higher Calling

cream, and other innovative coffee-based products. And since then Starbucks has continued to widen its range of product offerings, looking to enhance the coffee or beverage drinking experience within its stores and to attract more customers than the many millions who already come into its stores all around the world. And so, Starbucks now offers several blends of coffee; handcrafted coffee-based beverages; hot and iced teas; baked goods; granola bars; oatmeal; breakfast sandwiches; yogurts; energy drinks; breath mints; and even music CDs and other kinds of merchandise both in its stores and through other means of mass distribution outside of its stores.

I will note that this diversification in product offering has allowed Starbucks to traverse some rough business waters. It is the reason why Starbucks could survive a decline in coffee consumption in America during the '80s, when Americans turned to other kinds of drinks and especially teas and carbonated beverages like soda in increasing numbers. It is the reason why Starbucks could survive a decline in coffee exports during the '90s. It is one of the reasons why Starbucks could survive the competition of other large companies in the coffee market who were competing harder and harder by keeping prices low. It is one of the reasons why Starbucks could weather the storm of the 2008 economic recession in the United States. It is one of the reasons why Starbucks has thrived in almost every market it has entered and traded in around the world.[27] Indeed, it is important to note that Starbucks has not only managed to survive through these and other challenges but to thrive and expand despite them. Had it not been for Starbucks' aspiration to appeal to a broader range of target audiences through an expanded product line, however, it easily could have succumbed to these market challenges.

---

27. The only market entry that seems not to have worked well for Starbucks is Israel. And apparently it failed there due to a conflict between the standards Starbucks wanted to see and the standards the local business partners could deliver. Starbucks withdrew from the Israel market because it felt its brand could be compromised. For more on this matter, see Simmons's *My Sister's A Barista*, esp. 140.

And I find the yearly ledger to be very telling. In 2012 Starbucks reported that 63 percent of its revenue came from the sale of coffee-related items, meaning that as much as 37 percent of its revenue came from the sale of non-coffee related vendibles. In 2015 the company reported that 73 percent of its sales came from beverage sales specifically, meaning that 27 percent of Starbucks' sales were non-beverage related and of this percentage it was reported that 19 percent came from food sales.[28] These are sales, in other words, that would not have been available to Starbucks had it remained wedded to its original core business errand of being only a whole-bean and ground coffee retailer. And these figures of 37 percent, 27 percent, and 19 percent are not insignificant of course: they determine and make the difference between success and struggle, between prosperity and insolvency. But it is worth stressing that these additional sales, and the product line diversification that occasioned them, would not have been possible if it hadn't been for Starbucks' expanded vision and sense of mission regarding its core business to begin with. Starbucks went from seeing itself as being in the business of roasting and selling whole-bean and ground coffee, to seeing itself as being in the coffeehouse business, and then eventually to seeing itself as being in the food and beverage business more broadly. This expanded understanding in regard to the kind of business it wanted to be has allowed Starbucks to remain committed to its coffee core all while also expanding its core business to a far wider concentric circle that includes the other coffee-based beverages and products; the teas; the hot chocolates; the pastries; the yogurts; the oatmeal; the breakfast sandwiches; the lunchboxes, etc., etc., etc. Without this expansion in its sense of core business errand, Starbucks likely would still be what it was at first—a beloved local coffee bean store in Seattle—or perhaps even another casualty in the retailing world, rather than the global food and beverage company and the global brand it is today with more than twenty-three thousand stores worldwide. And this teaches us much about the power of an expansive vision

---

28. See "By the Numbers: 18 Interesting Starbucks Statistics" (March 2016).

Embracing a Greater, Higher Calling

and sense of vocational mission no matter the industry, business, or line of work we may be in.

What Has Starbucks to do with Theological Education?: Expanding the Horizons

Tertullian, the first important Latin Christian author, once caustically asked, "what has Athens to do with Jerusalem?"[29] This he did back in the early third century because he didn't think highly of the use of Greek philosophical idioms and ideas in the attempt to explicate Christian faith. Similarly, today I gather that some might derisively ask, what has Starbucks to do with theological education and/or with seminaries? Well, I actually think that many fruitful comparisons can be drawn between coffee and Starbucks on the one hand and theology and the work of seminaries on the other. But the particular comparison on which I want to focus relates to the matter of business or vocational identity and mission, and the need at times to expand one's definition and understanding of that identity and mission in order not only to appeal to but to contribute to a larger public and purpose.

I think that the sense of self and mission with which most freestanding seminaries tend to work is analogous to that of Starbucks at its start, at least in regards to narrowly defined mission parameters. Much as Starbucks once saw itself as being solely in the business of selling roasted coffee bean and ground coffee for home consumption, many of these seminaries tend to think of themselves as being mainly in the business of training parish ministers. Like Starbucks at the start, they have discovered or created a small niche and seek to carry on serving it well. The problem is that in the case of seminaries this niche has become too restrictive to allow for long-term survivability, let alone for growth, advancement, and wide-ranging influence. And this for the reasons I have mentioned previously. And so, as Starbucks was able to do, it is now necessary for freestanding Protestant seminaries to reconsider

---

29. See *Prescription Against Heretics* 7.9.

their core business or vocation in order to configure it in broader terms and, thus, to appeal to and to be of service to a wider public.

This wouldn't require a total reinvention of what theological education is nor of what seminaries are. It simply requires a broader view of the purpose of theological education and of the mission of seminaries. For example, there is no reason why seminaries cannot see themselves and present themselves as being in the business of educating moral and religious leaders for work across a variety of professions or vocations. This broader "business errand" or educational mission would include the preparation of ministers for the churches, of course, but it would also make room for the cultivation of educators; journalists; social service agents; public health workers; hospital, prison, military, and college/university chaplains; foreign-service officers; interfaith/multifaith group directors; UN and global NGO agents, and of conscientious citizens or residents who are interested in greater religious understanding. And there is no reason why our seminaries cannot see the ultimate goal of their theological education as being that of contributing to the process of building a more sacred, compassionate, just, and peaceful world through the study, assessment, interpretation, and judicious reconstruction of the symbols and ideals of a religious faith. In this widened vision of a seminary's educational mission and purpose, the goal of training ministers for the churches would not be lost or de-emphasized. It would remain, and even as an important part of a seminary's vocational identity and duty, but in this case as *one* element or instance of a bigger social, global, and religious project.

And I note that most seminaries already have a curricular structure in place that could support this broader sense of educational vision and mission. Yes, it is likely that some level of revisioning and retooling will be necessary to make sure that our courses and programs of study provide students with the resources and special training they need to successfully enter into the various fields or occupations I just mentioned. But the core education provided at most seminaries lends itself to the preparation of people for work across a variety of fields. The problem is that the applicability of a theological education is not often cast in these wider terms. That being so, few people learn of the broad value of a seminary theological education. And this is mostly because our seminaries see themselves as being primarily in the business of training ministers for the churches, and because this is the message they convey to the general public. And this is a major reason why freestanding seminaries are finding it so difficult to recruit new students. Basically, the issue is that they are fishing for new students in a small and rapidly shrinking student pool, and they are not presenting themselves in a sufficiently appealing way to a broader range of target audiences. The foremost task to which seminaries should turn their attention, therefore, is to the generation of a wider vision with regards to the broader applicability of a theological education and to the articulation of that vision more consistently on all occasions and in all forms of inner and outer communications—in recruitment paraphernalia; website information; open house functions; new student orientation events; career counseling sessions; convocation and commencement proceedings; trustee, faculty, and staff meetings, etc., etc. In short, all of the departments or offices of our seminaries, and all of the representatives who work within them, should try to get into the habit of consistently thinking and talking about theological education and about the mission and purpose of the seminary in these broader, grander terms.

Although my focus has mostly been in the area of appealing to a wider public and of attracting new students, it should be clear that the expansion I am calling for in regards to our understanding of the mission and purpose of a seminary theological education can help us to accomplish even more than this. I think it can help us to do better justice to the nature of theology itself. Theology is a wide-ranging, broadly relevant, and extremely interesting area of study. It deals with fundamental questions about the journey of life, and it attends to a wide range of terms, concepts, texts, stories, and practices created and developed in and through human processes of reflection on life and within the context of a religious faith for the purposes of providing meaning and orientation in life.

A field of study as deep, wide-ranging, and dynamic as this should not be limited to the aims of one profession, even for one as rich and complex as is the profession of pastoral ministry or ministry in general. Theology stands for more than what the churches say and do, and it stands for more than the practical pursuits of the profession of parish ministry or even of the profession of ministry more generally. For that reason, the theological education our freestanding Protestant seminaries provide should stand for more than this as well.

The broader definition of the mission and purpose of theological education I provided above could help our seminaries in two ways then. First, it could help them to appeal to a bigger public and to play a more vital role in the process of building a more sacred, compassionate, just, and peaceful world. Second, it could help them to embrace the rich complexity and wider significance of theology.

But the broader business errand I assigned to our Protestant freestanding seminaries is just one example of a way in which the mission and purpose of a seminary can be conceived of more broadly. Thinking of our seminaries as being in the business of educating moral and religious leaders for work across a variety of professions or vocations, and seeing their ultimate goal as being that of contributing to the process of building a more sacred, compassionate, just, and peaceful world is one way we can go. No doubt that there are many other ways in which we can think more broadly of the mission and purpose of the freestanding seminary. Some of these may be even more radical in thought than my rather modest proposal at missional redefinition. One way or the other, I am certain that those who work in or are affiliated with freestanding mainline Protestant seminaries will need to think of and speak of the mission and purpose of theological education more broadly and more creatively than they have tended to over the years. Signs of the need for such a redefinition are noticeable and plentiful. Simply put, freestanding mainline Protestant seminaries can no longer afford to continue seeing themselves as preacher/pastor factories. As noble as that calling has been and continues to be, it is now a good time for these schools to embrace a bigger and possibly even a higher calling.

Bibliography

Campbell, Ted. "Glory Days?" *The Christian Century* 131, no. 14 (2014), 11–13.

Chaves, Mark. *American Religion: Contemporary Trends.* Princeton, NJ: Princeton University Press, 2011.

Gryboski, Michael. "The Decline of Decline? Alarming Rate of Mainline Protestants Leaving Church May Be Slowing Down." *The Christian Post* (2014).

Henson, Greg, and Gary Hoag. "More Schools, Fewer Students: What's Your Seminary's Position in the Changing Market of Theological Education?" *In Trust* 25, no. 1 (2013) 16–17.

Hout, Michael, et al. "The Demographic Imperative in Religious Change in the United States." *American Journal of Sociology* 107, no. 2 (2009) 468–500.

Linder, Ellen W., ed. *Yearbook of American and Canadian Churches* (2009). http://www.yearbookofchurches.org/.

Miller, Glenn. *Piety and Intellect: The Aims and Purposes of Ante-Bellum Theological Education.* Atlanta: Scholars, 1990.

———. *Piety and Profession: American Protestant Theological Education, 1870–1970.* Grand Rapids: Eerdmans, 2007.

Ruger, Anthony, and Chris A. Meinzer. "Through Trial and Tribulation: Financing Theological Education 2001–2011." *Auburn Studies,* July 18, 2014, 1–24.

Wheeler, Barbara G., and Anthony T. Ruger. "Sobering Figures Point to Overall Enrollment Decline: New Research from the Auburn Center for the Study of Theological Education." *In Trust,* no. 3 (2013) 5–11.

Wheeler, Barbara G., et al. "Theological Student Enrollment: A Special Report from the Auburn Center for the Study of Theological Education." *Auburn Studies,* August 16, 2013, 1–21.

———. "How are We Doing? The Effectiveness of Theological Schools as Measured by The Vocation and Views of Graduates." *Auburn Studies,* December 13, 2007, 1–31.

4

A House Built on Sand?
A Blunt Look at the Assumptions of Theological Education

Nick Carter

I'M NOT SURE I can be optimistic about the future of theological education. Sure, I can say there will be *a* future to theological education. But what that will look like and whether seminaries as we have known them are in that future is problematic. Mission clarity, relevance, agility, cost, and the viability of the business model offer critical inflection points. Each needs a serious, if not blunt, conversation if we are to find any reason for optimism. Without it we may be swept away on the incoming tide.

From inside the world of theological education we are apt to lock arms and affirm the "need" for what we do; the rigorous preparation of clergy and other leaders for the church and society. Those of us who have received it, served in it, and observed the benefits of a "learned clergy," will (with a few caveats) eagerly applaud the "need" argument. We may even get a few "Amens" from the graying folks in the pews and the denominational bodies that still claim as "theirs" the children they all but abandoned a generation ago. But standing in the public square like Bill Murray in the movie "*What about Bob?*" shouting, "*I need. I need. I need,*" isn't going to get us very far.

If we are serious about the business of preparing faith leaders for the church and society, we have to examine our assumptions about what we think the church and society really needs from us. A hard look at the foundational concepts and designs that underlie what we do is essential if we are to survive the waves of a changing sea. Just what church is it that we are preparing folks to serve? Is it a church that existed fifty years ago, or worse, may have never existed? Then we have to candidly assess our economics and institutional structures by asking what may be the hardest question: How do justify the way we do business?

It's a harsh reality. According to the National Congregations Study (NCS)[1] at Duke, the median church size is now seventy-five; and the US Congregational Life Survey (USCLS)[2] tells us the average church size is 187. The higher average size is due to the concentration of worshippers in large churches, revealing that 50 percent of worshippers now attend 10 percent of the churches. Without a terribly deep examination of the levels of activity or pledging in those churches, it is clear that close to 70 percent of mainline Protestant churches can't support a full-time minister with benefits. Over 30 percent of churches have part-time ministers now.[3] In other words, there are dramatically fewer sustainable jobs in this market than a generation or two ago. If there aren't jobs in a profession, it won't attract candidates to that profession no matter how noble the calling or clever the advertising.

If this weren't enough, there are painful corollaries to the job problem. Seminaries are in an ethical trap regarding women in ministry. Those traditions that are open to it have seen a huge increase in female students and are working hard to recruit more. The dramatic rise of women in ministry over the last forty years

---

1. Chaves and Eagle, *Wave III*.

2. "Characteristics of U.S. Congregations, by faith group—part 1 (2008/2009)." U.S. Congregational Life Survey, Louisville, Kentucky.

3. MacDonald, "As Denominations Decline, Numbers of Unpaid Ministers Rise."

probably saved several seminaries (and churches!). But the job prospects for women in the church are still tough and seminaries have not made a matching commitment to fight for the placement of women. No jobs. In a related vein, the number of women on faculties, on boards, and in the office of president or dean lags well behind the demographics of who is buying what we are selling. No jobs. On the other side of the coin is the surge in Latino/a population and yet their notably small enrollment numbers in seminary (highest in evangelical Protestant schools). Hispanics comprise barely 5 percent of US seminary students yet they represent 17.6 percent of the US population.[4] Missed job opportunity. The black church has better news on some fronts, (for instance, it has understood bivocation almost since its inception), but it is not immune to the same issues. On top of all this is a ministerial profession that has not been robing itself in glory of late, which has resulted in a rather unattractive brand position. Apart from the gift of Pope Francis, Rev. William Barber in North Carolina, or Jim Wallis at Sojourners, when is the last time you read a story or saw a movie about the moral rectitude of a minister or priest? Is it any wonder that seminaries are apoplectic about their recruiting numbers?

As theologues who are assessing the church we must also look at the society of which the church is a part. What society is it from which we draw our candidates and into which we send our graduates? We live in a postmodern, deconstructionist, wired, post-Christian, and increasingly post-factual age (or at least one of "alternative facts"). No longer is the church a beneficiary of the society around it. Institutions are viewed with rising suspicion and the public's hypocrisy detectors are turned all the way up when they examine us religious types. Millennials (the target group for every seminary recruiter) are shapers of modern culture, and notably they are not joiners, which have forced churches (and seminaries) to struggle with their old assumptions about what "membership," "enrollment," and "stewardship" means in a postmodern age.

---

4. Association of Theological Schools, 2015–16 Annual Data Tables and the US Census Bureau, American Fact Finder, July 2015.

Then too, the distorted nature of an advanced consumer society is omnipresent, and helpless churches are swept up in it. The average family shops for a church today just like they shop for a car or a TV—usually beginning on the Internet (a realm where most churches are bumpkin-ish). The critical factors in their decision-making about a church have more to do with services offered than denominational identity. Church "customers" want to know if there is child-care, a youth program, and, of course, parking. Their approaches to stewardship, sadly, increasingly echo a consumer "fee for service" mentality. Seminaries would also be well advised to pay attention to this phenomenon, as students adopt a sharper consumer mind-set when it comes to enrollment and course content.

One of the greatest determining factors in selecting a church (right behind sermons) is the sense of community, welcome, and belonging prospective members find there[5] (and given this centrality, one wonders what course seminarians can take on how to build a church community?). Everyone is aware of the rise of the "nones" (no religious affiliation—now 25–30 percent of the population), and of the 85 percent of them who say they are still spiritual in some sense. They search for an "authentic," "welcoming," and "spiritual" connection.[6] As elusive as these things are to pin down, it seems like our future needs to give more attention to such realities.

And, lest you think we are done talking about society's influence, take careful note that "truth" and "facts" have been all but tarred and feathered and run out of town. What used to be our sweet spot has turned rather lemony, hasn't it? Like the family radio the ten-year-old has figured out how to dismantle, but has no clue or interest in putting back together, the church today has been deconstructed by the society around it and gummed up with

5. "Choosing a New Church or House of Worship" Pew Research Center, Religion and Public Life, August 23, 2016; and National Church Life Survey (Australia), Healthy Churches, Connections for Life, NCLS Research, North Sydney, NSW (2016).

6. "Nones' on the Rise," Pew Research Center, Religion and Public Life, October 9, 2012.

consumerism such that the average seminary grad has little preparation for coping.

Since their inception seminaries have sought to be responsive to the changing needs of church and society. The same is true today. Most of the topics I've mentioned are ones with which the faculties of theological schools, denominational officials, and pastors are struggling now. Yet, the consequences are substantial and complex, thus it is no wonder the search for solutions carries on at a speed akin to cancer research (one day we pray they will figure it out). Meanwhile, one-third of seminaries are in financial trouble and another third while stable today could easily be in trouble tomorrow. A large endowment isn't an answer to a broken business model. A taxi with a full tank of gas but no customers is just a parked car.

Given these realities, and my colleagues know there are many more, how shall we speak of the *future* of theological education? We will be quick to theologize and biblicize over each of these challenges to our sacred turf. We'll talk of the nature of the church and ministry, and the need to stand prophetically over against society. We'll even look back over the history of the church, and smartly ask "What is God doing in this time?" Defensively we'll point to our initiatives in bi-vocational ministry, the competency-based curricula, online education and, and . . . But in the end far too many of us will gloss over the more fundamental problems— like a viable business model—and propose "fixes" to a Barnum and Bailey business model when we live in a Cirque de Soleil age. Many mourn the passing of the old circus, but too few see their schools reflected in that story.

The reality is that, other than the gospel itself, almost every one of the assumptions upon which theological education in the US has been based for the last 200 years is in the midst of being swept away. Whether we look at the broader idea of theological education or we look specifically at seminaries, we end up in the same place. What we teach, how we teach it, who teaches it, where we teach, and to whom we teach is all undergoing radical change (as does who teaches us!). Sure, a few of the righteous will react with indignation pounding the table as they say the Bible, theology, and history are unchanged and enduring. But as issues of race, ethnicity, gender, and class deconstruct the texts, expand theology, and rewrite history, we have to ask which part they think is unchanged and enduring. This doesn't even begin to address the issues of interfaith perspectives on the Christian claims to truth, or how one teaches, learns, and gives witness to one's confession in a pluralistic and rapidly globalizing world. We cannot run from any of these challenges lest we invite the worst condemnation that can be leveled at our faith: irrelevance.

A gaggle of gifted scholars are working on answers to these questions and we are blessed by their insights,[7] so I hope they aren't too defensive. But (perhaps like a dentist spraying cold water in a cavity) one must ask: will those insights pay the bills? We can no longer ignore the question of sustainability. To begin it will be necessary, I think, to include two additional topics to our inquiries: money and institutions—heretofore subjects on the margins of discussion. There is a direct connection between how we think about money in theological education and our understanding of how seminaries and churches run. Similarly neglected is a theology of institutions—how they are fallen and how they might be redeemed. Our future depends on revisiting these vital issues: we ignore them at our peril. It may seem crass to urge this, but I would also argue that without a look at the business side of our sacred enterprise we invite a troubled future. Business models are proved on the basis of a product or solution profitably sold to a customer with a satisfaction level that engenders repeat business in market large enough to justify further investment. The nature of our business is flawed: we have to sell at a discount because our production costs are too high for the customer and must be subvented, our market is shrinking, and we have decreasing evidence of satisfied customers. The failure of theological education's business model has consequences for everything we do or hope to do in the future.

---

7. Stephen Graham's work at ATS on *Educational Models and Practices* (which I discuss below) with eighteen peer groups working on a major report for the 2018 ATS Biennial, is notable in this regard.

See how the business problem cascades. If the basic business model of theological education is broken, what shall we assume, for instance, about the future support for scholarship? As seminaries inevitably close and merge, there are fewer teaching positions. And as seminary administrators wrestle with their ongoing budget crises (and even those who don't), the prospect of using contingent faculty looks increasingly attractive. It may have a solid financial benefit, but the cost to sustained scholarship is enormous. Contingent faculties aren't as committed to, supported in, or freed for scholarship. Where's the future in that?

Denominations have to be confronted about the scholarship issue as well. Other than our Roman Catholic (and perhaps a few Lutheran) colleagues, decreasing numbers see the connection between solid scholarship in their faith tradition and denominational identity. How many Protestant denominationally affiliated seminaries have scholars of their tradition researching and securing their unique confessions in light of the contemporary upheaval in the church? Those denominations that still manage to give money to "their" seminaries see the bulk of it spent on property and maintenance—not on scholars and scholarships. There is hardly a confession today that isn't facing the threat of theologically "free range" clergy redefining their tradition. Just look at the convulsions within the Baptist family where scores of rebel leaders are advocating decidedly un-Baptist positions and policies, bending that rich history to accommodate their social and political views by dressing them up with biblical fig leaves. "Soul Freedom" has been locked up and the key thrown away.

When I look at seminaries specifically, there are even greater challenges to our assumptions. There are about 210 seminaries in the US and about 72,000 students (down from 80,000 ten years ago).[8] That suggests an average of about 333 students per school, but the reality is that 50 percent of the students attend roughly 10 percent of the schools and of those 90 percent are conservative evangelical schools. Forty percent of seminaries have declining enrollments and only 20 percent are growing. Looking closer at those

---

8. Association of Theological Schools, "State of the Industry" 2015 webinar.

who are officially "growing," we see many whose finances are not any better off, as seminary tuition rarely covers more than 30 percent of the cost of educating a student. More students look good on the headcount metrics, but they also mean more fundraising. In this business model merely having more students isn't necessarily an answer for the future.

A typical seminary is trapped in another old assumption: a residential student body. When a little over 200 years ago Andover Seminary introduced the model for the "modern" seminary, it led the way with a graduate three-year model combined with a residential faculty and a residential student body. It was cutting edge stuff. Now as Andover Newton packs its bags to relocate to New Haven, it leaves in its wake five dormitories it could no longer fill. Yes, enrollment was down, but of the 200 students that were still there only about 30 percent actually lived on campus. An older student demographic, the trend toward bi-vocational options, and the advent of online courses made dormitories an anachronism. This, coupled with crippling maintenance costs, the challenge of keeping current with accessibility codes, and the conundrum of ensuring contemporary Internet connectivity for the wired student body (I won't mention parking), makes for a deadly formula.

Here's another assumption that has exploded: the cost of theological education. The seminary model most of us employ was originally designed on the assumption of it being tuition free or at most provided at a nominal affordable cost. For all the innovative ideas we may engender in this exercise about the future of our discipline, if we don't have an answer to the cost of it, we are wasting our time. Ministry occupies a unique position among the professions. We require the most training for the least prospect of financial reward of any profession. We demand training like lawyers and, at best, compensation like elementary school teachers. And, more than any graduate institution, seminaries can't balance their budgets on the backs of students because it undermines our mission. Too many of our graduates are leaving the ministry not because they have lost their faith, but because they can't pay off their student debt. The result is that seminaries have to be quite sophisticated and aggressive about fundraising and other revenue generating efforts in order to make up the 70–80 percent of the cost of the education students can't pay. Here again, 90 percent of our profession is all but naïve about the staggering demands of fundraising upon our presidents and boards to close that gap.

So if that's the reality, what's in store for the future? A great deal will depend on seminary leadership: presidents, boards, and faculties. Other places we might look are simply not capable of making the critical difference in our future. I don't believe the denominations will be much help. They are generally too weak financially, ingrown, or busy with internecine warfare to have the insight and courage to abandon a siege-like mentality and invest again in "their" seminaries. Besides, most seminaries have been weaned from denominational support for decades and have had to look elsewhere for sustenance. Those few who still offer some support have been decreasing the amount year after year as their own resources wane. Then too, many Protestant seminaries have only a fraction of students who are from their tradition—even though many still carry the denominational name in their title. Geography and price are often bigger factors. Granted, some traditions demand attendance at a denominationally affiliated school, but there is not a lot of evidence that this "circle the wagons" model is working either, as it often lacks the deeper commitment to what seminaries really need to address their financial issues.

The Association of Theological Schools (ATS) isn't really in a position to come to the rescue either. For all the good it does (which is a lot), it is not a very agile institution. ATS is in the standards business and those standards are all but leaden when it comes to the discovery of new models. Granted, in recent years ATS has begun to loosen up a bit. The best work in this area may be Stephen Graham's project on *Educational Models and Practices*, which hopes to not only issue a major report at the 2018 ATS Biennial, but make recommendations for a revision in standards that will be more accommodating to innovation. But for all the strength of the content and design focus that this admirable effort promises, one worries if the business dimension of these new models is being examined as much as it should. Sustainability is an urgent issue. As Robert Landrebe's recent insightful article in *In Trust* points out, new models can take up to six years to prove viability.[9] We need to be exploring new models, but we have to keep our eye on the prize and shout: "Show me the money!" Beyond block and tackle work of accreditation, the ATS's best stuff is in the practical seminars it offers for seminary leaders (the program for presidents is excellent) and their data sharing (which I suspect is underutilized). Not too long ago the ATS did a great service for several schools that were in financial difficulty by bringing them together for some intensive work on their fiscal health. But this valuable counsel doesn't—and can't—address the market in which our businesses run or the degree to which the scores of standards we must meet each come with a price tag and that to remain accredited demands an unstated level of sustained financial investment. If this weren't enough, some schools must be accredited twice (once by ATS and again by a federal regional body)—each exercise being heavily duplicative and costly for the school being scrutinized. In the world of accreditation opportunities for innovation are rare and doing something out of the norm has to be viewed with a skeptical eye. Valued partners, yes; but the future is probably not here.

And the future of theological education isn't going to come from the foundations, either. Those who fund seminaries are few and we claw over them (and each other) like thirsty souls who find an oasis in the desert. To be sure, they deserve plenty of credit for what they have been able to do. They have been taking risks with us for a long time, and we are blessed by it. Given our current circumstance, though, I wish they'd take more risks. But other than hot-housing bold experiments, they really can't be the solution to the future. Two suggestions: 1) Foundations could put tougher requirements for demonstrating long-term sustainability of projects into the guidelines for their grants; 2) more seminary presidents ought to talk directly with program officers as much for perspective and wisdom as they do begging for dollars.

---

9. Landrebe, "Creating Your Future Seminary."

Finally, those who offer consulting advice, research, and assistance—like *In Trust*, Center for the Study of Theological Education (at Auburn Seminary), The Hartford Institute, The Forum for Theological Education, the Center for Congregations, and Wabash—deserve a nod. Notably Barbara Wheeler and Tony Ruger, our in-house physicians, have opened our eyes, documented our challenges, and counseled many a troubled school. For the most part these consulting organizations—just like family doctors—do fine work, see many of our issues up close, and have insights we need to listen to. That said, one wishes they would give greater urgency to seminary business models. In any case, it is unfortunate that their efforts are too often rescue work, and one worries about the sustainability of their own business models (witness the story of the Alban Institute). If it weren't for the foundations, many of them would be out of business. They are good doctors, coaches, and counselors, but they don't have to run the race—we do.

Add all this up and here's the bottom line: theological schools must realize that in the end no one is going to save them but themselves. If so, the challenge becomes whether or not seminary leaders, who hold the mission of the school in their trust, will be able to envision a bold and financially viable future that is free from old assumptions before the boat sinks. For some it is already too late, and for those who are deluding themselves by bailing a hopelessly leaky boat, it engenders sadness. They have grown comfortable with wet feet and have forgotten that bailing is not missional. The problem is that change does not come without a clear sense of urgency, and generating that in an academic institution is a glacial exercise. The metaphor begs the analogy to global warming, which is apt. The message is clear: complacency is eroding our seminaries. And in complacency is where we look most foolish. We have always had trouble discerning the difference between being a fool for Christ and being a plain fool.

Here are a few thoughts. First and foremost, the future of theological education will hinge on a revitalized understanding of mission. Trustees and faculties must get in the habit of regularly and honestly asking, "How do we know we are accomplishing our mission?" and not accepting warm and fuzzy anecdotal evidence as an answer. The assessment movement is forcing faculties to look harder at the effectiveness of their efforts in the classroom, but it has yet to have a measurable impact in the board room where the culture of assessment begins and ends. If governing bodies spent more time looking at their financials with a missional and theological eye, they might be motivated to make bolder decisions about focusing their efforts and confronting things like deferred maintenance costs. Faculties, for their part, need to begin to measure not merely outcomes at the end of a class, but outcomes three and five years after graduation. Together the seminary leadership needs to value mission—their reason for existence—in more tangible ways than they ever have. Are we actually accomplishing what we set out to do?

The future also demands a quantum leap in interconnectedness. If we are all in the business of advancing the realm of God, then we need a dramatic upgrade in mutuality. Theological education of the future has to be a shared enterprise. Alone few seminaries can afford to provide contemporary graduate level accredited education, pay staff and scholars, meet all the federal, state, and local requirements, be responsive to their many stakeholders, offer quality IT, and maintain campuses on the revenue they are generating. The business model doesn't work. The sooner we face that reality the better our future will be.

Interconnectivity means that we must be open to creative partnerships whose first prerequisite is institutional ego disarmament, a willingness to give up control of some things, and find new levels of trust upon which we can work together. It is a higher calling, not surrender.

In some parts of the country we might be well served to have a regional administrative "hub and spokes" approach to what we do—particularly when it comes to administration. Part of our leaky boat problem is that we religious types insist on hiring and elevating administrators who are theologically and academically trained, but have little skill in the business of running an institution of higher learning. Why hire someone who is trained as an electrician to do your plumbing? If you want a well-run business, hire an experienced business person or at least someone who has had substantial training in that side of the equation! An administrative hub run by business professionals in finance, IT, financial aid, HR, and even maintenance would be a breath of fresh air. Any number of schools could benefit from a property management corporation that would let them stop trying to do something at which they aren't all that good.

Another take on this is a "university" model, with various schools, each with its own dean. Here the institutional ego problem raises its head again: What if my seminary didn't have a president? In many cases it would be a good thing! That said, I am not entirely convinced embedding in an existing secular university is the best solution, because, while the financial foundation may be secure, contemporary universities are increasingly uninterested in ministry other than as a specimen to be dissected and examined. Now, to counter that point, there may be enough old restricted endowment money (raised when ministry was revered) that binds the university in a way that will avoid this threat, but I'd look closely at what is happening in those schools before I concluded they were the best choice. I suspect that most university presidents are secretly trying to find ways to redirect that money.

Consortia offer another variation in this realm. They have had some success in cross registration, but haven't exactly dazzled us with shared services and or lasting business benefit. Long-established consortia like the Boston Theological Institute (BTI) and Graduate Theological Union (GTU) have admirable features, but they often stumble over their own academic aspirations and lose sight of the founding mission of strengthening the member schools. That's why a purely business service model makes more sense; it will be judged solely on the quality of its services to the partners and its own financial health. I'd love to see the emergence of a serious business with a missional heart dedicated to solving some of the hardest financial and administrative issues schools face that sells its services to seminaries at a rate that works for both. It might attract some able business leaders who are at the point in their careers where they'd like to move from "success to significance" and take on something like this.

And something else: We must stop deluding ourselves about our physical campuses. Many schools verge on idolatry over their property, and are regularly sucked into a nostalgic black hole by their alums. What is there about the future of theological education that is arterially tied to buildings, boilers, and quadrangles? Little. Deferred maintenance has to be seen for what it is; an institutional cancer, often metastasizing unseen until it is too late. If there is to be a seminary of the future it has to be far more agile and less chained to its capital assets. The weight of tradition and the blinding romance of a physical "institution" are as threatening to schools as they are to churches. They seduce us away from our mission, and seminaries end up as lousy teachers in what they model to their graduates about physical assets. It's no wonder ministers are so flummoxed over their own aging buildings.

Sure, we need classrooms, but we could benefit from a far more imaginative definition of what they are. In a technological age the possibilities are enormous. We are still infants in the online learning world and we need to grow up fast. In part we need to better prepare our students for the wired ministry they will be called upon to perform. We need to take advantage of the true opportunity technology presents and become more sophisticated in our pedagogies than online courses have demonstrated us so far. MOOCs, learning centers, TED lectures, and "world learning" (e.g. the University of London's International Program of flexible study) are opening exciting doors. We've made good moves in the areas of competency models, but blended, truly interdisciplinary and more individualized pedagogies are needed. We also need to get over our simplistic critique of the online world. Faculty love to complain about the loss of the personal touch, the lack of human community, and the extra work of online courses and interactions. The reality is that an entire generation—the one we want to come to seminary—lives online, has already found a community online, and takes most of its social cues from the World Wide Web.

We can get good counsel from other disciplines here. Places like the Center for Innovative Teaching and Learning (Indiana University at Bloomington—IUB) and Harvard's Innovation Lab (HIL) could be interesting partners for seminaries. We forget that, despite the good work of folks at Wabash, our professors, while competent scholars, may be mediocre teachers. Most were never required to take a teaching methods course, are supervised by someone who never took one, and, at best, may only be modeling how they were taught. At places like IUB they could be exposed to contemporary methods, classroom design and use, as well as new ideas in contextual learning. At places like HIL seminary professors might be bitten by the entrepreneurial spirit of problem solving and teamwork that could invigorate our ideas of leadership. A dialogue with sister professions who are dealing with many of the same cultural phenomenons could bear fruit, as Stephen Graham points out in his ATS blog about law schools.[10]

It would be fun if, for instance, the Lilly Endowment or the Luce Foundation would fund the creation of a state-of-the-art learning lab for theological education. Seminaries could send faculty there for in-service training, be exposed to master teachers, examine their own pedagogies (andragogies?!), and network with colleagues in state-of-the-art colloquia. The lab could have all the latest smart equipment, software training sessions, and innovative classroom designs. Given the advances in technology, it would even be possible for a learning lab class to "drop in" on a master teacher halfway across the country and observe her at work and, with a head mic and earphone, even interact with her as she works.

I can't leave the topic of classroom without addressing the issue of a global classroom. We all recognize the opportunity and urgency of a globalizing society—even ATS has developed standards in this area! Yet, few seminaries are doing more than student and faculty exchanges, mission trips, and "partnerships" with seminaries or religious bodies in other countries. I think we

---

10. ATS: January 13, 2017 blog entry, "Law schools and theological schools: learning together," http://www.ats.edu/blog/educational-models-and-pactices/law-schools-and-theological-schools-learning-together.

could be far more creative, particularly when one considers the prohibitive costs associated with most of these programs. Why not begin by having faculty exchange syllabi with their colleagues in other countries? It could invite a fascinating dialogue about cross-cultural learning and scholarship, and perhaps even make a statement about overcoming First World bias. Why not connect students and faculty electronically, long before someone buys a $1,500 airline ticket? Students could study texts together, pray together, and share papers through email or Skype. Apps like Google Translate make this increasingly possible.

The future of theological education must also think more boldly in regard to accessibility. Physical accessibility is the narrowest definition. I think the future will demand the creation of a "passport to theological education" built around an idea of "study anywhere, anytime." Breaking down the barriers to admission to seminary, which now require a bachelor's degree (or exceptions in a small number of cases), a passport model could fling open the doors and dramatically increase our ability to serve marginalized and underserved communities. It also provides a nifty tool for serving an increasingly mobile student population. Upon adequate recommendation and review, anyone could matriculate at a seminary and be issued an ID and a "passport" (an official barrier-free transcript) that will be stamped every time the student takes a course, a workshop, or a recognized learning module. A post-matriculation "readiness" diagnostic and assessment could give an advisor a read on recommending a course of study. As s/he meets various thresholds in the journey the student will be awarded recognition (certificates, diplomas, etc.). In the process, the student can legitimately claim to be enrolled in a seminary, but is free to find and secure an education in a host of places and at an affordable price. The controlling factor is that the seminary faculty and administrators will have to approve the learning opportunities, much like most continuing education models (and receive a fee for doing so). Placing the seminary and the faculty at the center of approval of individuals and programs safeguards against offerings of marginal value or poorly prepared leaders, but ensures them a closer relationship to the denominational entities that offer (widely varying) training opportunities. It will be an added load for the faculty, but the payoff could be great. It also makes the theological enterprise a dynamic and market-driven exercise, which demands constant innovation.

The added benefit from the passport model is that all students have the same standing, the only difference being relative progress on the journey. Importantly, the passport could be recognized as a lifelong learning tool. Far too many clergy graduate from seminary, are ordained, lead congregations, and teach others, without being required to read another book or take another course. Denominations and churches could raise standards of professional promotion and placement based on the continual accumulation of "stamps" in the passport—not all of which have to be degrees or even formal seminary courses.

A word needs to be added here about the movement in recent years within denominations to introduce "alternatives" to ordination (i.e., theological education). In particular it was an attempt to respond to frustrations of marginalized and underserved constituencies, recognizing that not everyone is able to enter graduate theological study (or afford it), yet these folks were being called on to lead churches. The analysis of the problem was good; the solution was terrible. What it did was create a path around the seminaries and call upon those who have no training for it to take the place of seminary faculty to discern skill and readiness for ministry. Those who have been a part of these alternative systems regularly despair over the flaws in the model. Rather than skirting the seminaries, the denominations should have turned to the seminaries and held them accountable to design an effective response. The current design is a sure path to a decidedly unlearned clergy. And the seminaries themselves—if they are to have a future—need to stop whining about these flawed designs and the lowering of standards, and make solving this problem one of their top priorities.

Here's something else to consider: We need to model what we teach. A key extension of the mutuality argument above, our collective future must find a way to revisit and reappropriate our ideas of what it means to be "evangelical" and builders of the "Beloved Community." We have to broaden the meaning of these words to encompass the wide spectrum of the Christian family and find ways to better model God's love in how we interact with each other. The divisions that have torn the church asunder in the last generations are tragic and an embarrassment. While we have exhausted ourselves standing in judgment over one another, we have done little to give witness to God's realm on earth. If anything, we collectively stand in dock before a cynical postmodern generation who sees little more than hypocrisy and pettiness in us. Our future must have a new understanding of the authenticity of faith if our claims to truth are to have any weight. That can only happen if we figure out how to rise above the meanness and smallness of our social Bible battles and refocus on having some genuine Good News to share. Bridge-building or "border-crossing" skills have to be a part of every seminary curriculum.

There is another side to evangelism that needs some work. It is the entrepreneurial and "tent making" dimension of ministry. Here our conservative colleagues have a few things to teach the rest of us. It does us no good if our students graduate thinking they have a corner on the truth, if they don't have a clue about the institutional physics of launching a program, revitalizing a church, or worse, actually starting a church. Without these things their truth becomes an abandoned child. How does one create an "irresistible force" to overcome the physics of something that is not moving? How do we overcome the bad math of more churches closing than are opening? Only with a renewed appreciation of the Pauline and entrepreneurial dimensions of our work is this possible.

A word now on the topic of libraries. It is clear that the future of theological education will have to address the question of libraries. We watch with dismay as new classes of students (and new generations of scholars) use the library less and less, doing most of their work online. Culture, convenience, and cost are all factors. We are in a hybrid moment now, as schools scramble to straddle the two cultures of acquisition and access. Clearly, the future lies with the latter. The first challenge is to get to that future before the transition bankrupts us.

The future I see (an idea stolen from gifted colleagues) is that of a technology driven "knowledge center," much like an Apple Store with its "Apple Geniuses" on staff. Helping students and scholars access the information they need, navigating and finding resources, which will be largely digital, becomes the primary mission of the library of the future. Groups like the Online Computer Library Center (www.OCLC.org) are offering insights of which more of us need to take advantage. The storage of texts and artifacts is an increasingly museum-like function. While necessary for some dimensions of research, it is fading in importance to the regular operation of the school but still carries huge costs. That's why facilities for the storage of hard copy materials can and should be consolidated and jointly financed. Accreditation standards also need more flexibility to facilitate this change and free seminaries from the physicality of buildings and stacks, particularly in regard to remote centers.

The final topic I want to touch upon with regards to the future of seminaries may be the one on which the rest hinge: financial viability. As noted throughout this essay, the failing seminary business model may be our biggest challenge on the road to the future. Divinity schools that are part of large universities may escape, as may those independent schools with large endowments. But even those who elude the problem today will still have a reckoning with the fundamental challenges to our assumptions, our design, and the disappearing market for what we do.

Most seminaries have fine CFOs, accounting teams, and development officers. But accurate and timely reports on the fact that you are losing money and eating up your endowment do not chart a path to a viable future. Many CFOs do their good work only to watch as presidents and boards of trustees fail to understand the long-term import of those numbers.

Central to rethinking the business model are two fundamental issues. First we have to look at the fact that seminaries today are functioning in a saturated "red ocean" of competitors.[11] We are clones of each other in too many ways. And we all know that there are too many seminaries for this market, so we have fallen into a Darwinian fix, competing for a limited number of students. So oriented, the future demands that some of us merge, embed, or go out of business. Unfortunately, the fear of and resistance to doing so, along with the blindness to true financial circumstance, are burning up millions of dollars of endowment money and making the most unwelcome outcomes inevitable.

For those that have a chance at surviving a sea change in entrepreneurial thinking is essential. What's missing in many cases is the differentiation, agility, and low cost needed in order to succeed. The challenge is not battling other schools as competitors, but that of creating "blue oceans" of untapped new market spaces. Here the lessons come from businesses like Cirque de Soleil and Marvel, each of whom reinvented themselves and created new markets. Looking at businesses for inspiration and insight may at first seem antithetical to church minds, but if we look we'll see there is plenty of biblical evidence for such strategic thinking.

Second, we have to look again at the market. Yes, we have to look to the churches and what they want, but if we are focused on them exclusively we are missing large market segments that include the life of faith and the search for meaning. From the business side the question is, "Who is your customer?" There isn't a lot of evidence that seminaries know the answer to that one. New markets and alternative careers are emerging that seminaries are well positioned to serve, if we are clear about the customer question. By looking again at the definitions of "The Church" (vs. "church") and "ministry" we may allow ourselves to discover untapped markets of people who have previously rejected us or never considered us. For instance, the connections between health, aging, and spirituality are exploding with possibilities. I think there is also an exciting territory in the marriage of the growing interest in service to the poor (both domestic and international)

---

11. What follows is the argument laid out in Kim and Mauborgne, *Blue Ocean Strategy*.

and our legacy of missions. If we look we'll see a new generation of "passionaries"[12] who are interested in a life of service. It could be an enormous market. This is, perhaps, why so many schools have been looking at other degree and certificate programs than the Master of Divinity, which more than a decade ago began to be called into question as the "gold standard." The Master of Divinity requires three years of graduate study and tens of thousands of dollars to qualify for a profession that is mired in assumptions and designs that are generations out of date. How can we get students out sooner and then stay in relationship with them as they struggle with issues that we who taught them never knew would arise? A changing world demands an agile ministry, which can only come from an agile institution.

Conclusion

There is plenty of reason to be pessimistic given the state of things, but there still can be an exciting future for theological education. The future depends on whether we are prepared to shake off our complacency and urgently go to work on the issues that are truly critical to our survival. As my friend Rev. William Sloane Coffin was fond of saying, "We have to recognize what's staring us in the face before it hits us in the face." What's staring at us is a broken business model. Our assumptions are misplaced and out of date, particularly the assumptive model of the church and society for which we are preparing leaders. We have to design a better business model that can serve our mission but is also built on a foundation that is sustainable, which probably means that we have to get insight and help from other disciplines outside the church. Agility is essential, as is a willingness to let go of the things that keep us from being so. And above all, we need to model a theology of institutions, joy, and mutuality that offers an authentic witness to the radical nature of God's love. If we fail to do so, we have built our future on a house of sand (Matt 7:26).

---

12. A term borrowed from Barbara Metzler. See www.passionaries.com.

Bibliography

Chaves, Mark, and Alison Eagle. *Wave III: Religious Congregations in 21st Century America*. Durham, NC: Department of Sociology, Duke University, 2015.

Kim, W. Chan, and Renee Mauborgne. *Blue Ocean Strategy, Expanded Edition: How to Create Uncontested Market Space and Make the Competition Irrelevant*. Cambridge, MA: Harvard Business Review Press, 2015.

Landrebe, Robert S. "Creating Your Future Seminary." *In Trust New Year* 28, no. 2 (2017) 8–11.

MacDonald, G. Jeffrey. "As Denominations Decline, Numbers of Unpaid Ministers Rise." *Religion News Service* (2013).

5

From Resistance to Resurrection
Meadville Lombard's TouchPoint^{SM} *Model of Theological Education*[1]

SHARON WELCH AND MICHAEL S. HOGUE

Introduction

WHEN THE EXPRESSION "CHANGE or die" becomes a cliché, we should know there's something deeply wrong with denominational seminaries.[2]

Institutional change is difficult in any kind of institution, given that most institutions are structured in inherently conservative ways. Even the most liberal institutions, *qua* institutions, are driven fundamentally by a will to conserve and transmit their status quo. Yet when it comes to denominational seminaries, generic institutional resistance to change is magnified three times over. This seems to be a result of the tendency to idolatry in seminaries,

---

1. This is a revised version of an essay that appeared previously in *Theological Education* 48.2 (2014) 33–42.

2. Important studies providing context for this claim include Wheeler et al., "How are We Doing?," and Wind and Wood, *Becoming a Pastor*.

the peculiarities of theological educators as an academic subspecies, and the mystic nostalgia of alumni. Let us explain.

As religious institutions, seminaries are sometimes seduced by the idolatry that "the way we do things" is ultimately the way things should be done. The tendency in seminaries to transmute the status quo into an ultimate concern is part of what makes resistance to change in seminaries so *fanatical*, (or *enthusiastical*, as we liberals used to put it). This fanaticism is further compounded by the fact that seminaries tend to be populated by *faculties*. It just seems to be in the nature of most theological faculties to resist institutional change. Perhaps this is because they belong to a relatively clever but generally impractical human subspecies that is oblivious to its own material conditions. Of course this is only worsened if a majority of faculty members are *tenured* (whether by works or by grace seems to be a committee decision). In any event, with faculties in the picture, *fanatical* resistance becomes *fanatically reified*. It wouldn't seem that changing a seminary could become any more difficult, but it can. Consider the *alumni*. The alumni's very identity has been formed by some form of mystical experience described as "the-way-things-were-done-when-we-were-students." Thus when the alumni are taken into account, the result is *fanatically reified resistance, on stilts*.

Of course it doesn't have to be this way. After all, rather than being univocal, how a seminary responds to the imperative to "change or die" depends on its functional soteriology. At the seminary where we teach in Chicago, Meadville Lombard Theological School, our soteriology would be considered (euphemistically) dysfunctional by various traditional standards—after all, we're Unitarian Universalist. While in certain times and places this would no doubt have its disadvantages, it turns out that with respect to institutional change it has its benefits: when we face death, we have to really, really take it seriously.

So at Meadville Lombard when it became clear that we needed to "change or die" we chose to do what we could to change, and not simply incrementally. We went down to the bone and with fear and trembling took it upon ourselves to completely reshape our educational model. Our enrollment was shrinking nearly as fast as our endowment was being drawn down. Our physical plant was deteriorating. The antiquated boiler that heated our building quit in January, in Chicago! And yet, as a forward-looking bunch of religious liberals, we chose to face our circumstances squarely and bravely and to apply our best and most creative thinking to our various problems. We brought aboard the best consultants we knew and collaborated (nonviolently) to undertake a gut-rehab and "flip" our pending death into new life. While our soteriology may be unorthodox, we're happy to confirm that there *is* new life on the other side of change. This is our story.

Approaching Change: Methods and Theses

The first thing that should be said about Meadville Lombard's approach to change is that it was facilitated by the leadership of our President, Rev. Dr. Lee Barker, and our Provost, Dr. Sharon Welch (this is true, whether or not it gets us a raise). Their methodology of change reflected their catalytic style of leadership. They didn't impose a program onto the faculty. Instead they trusted in creative collaboration. But this wasn't an ungrounded trust. It was rooted in the priority they knew we all gave, and continue to give, to our school's mission—educating students in the Unitarian Universalist tradition in order to bring into the world our vision of justice, equity, and compassion. Our change methodology was thus missionally rooted in a common desire to develop an educational model worthy of our churches, our students, and the world they were being formed to serve.

It is also important to say that our methodology compelled us to reach out to work with and learn from others, rather than to try going it alone. We were, and continue to be, well aware of our limitations. At many different points we consulted with seasoned senior UU ministers, denominational leaders, educational assessment specialists, present and former students, and with colleagues from other theological schools. And in light of our understanding of the moral ambiguity of institutions, we also organized meetings to listen and learn from the experiences of students, educators, scholars, and religious professionals of color. Since even the most well-intentioned institutions can be vectors of oppression, we committed ourselves to meeting regularly with and holding ourselves accountable to racially and culturally diverse and socially marginalized friends and colleagues.

These shared commitments—to collaboration, mission, and accountability—framed several hypotheses about how to rebuild our educational model. The first of these was the idea that *there is no formula for ministry*.[3] What we meant by this was that ministry is less about the depositing of knowledge and skills than about the formation of particular dispositions.[4] To be an effective progressive religious leader in today's world, to be equipped to serve the ideals of justice, equity, and compassion, requires, among other dispositions, the eagerness to work across boundaries of cultural and other forms of difference; the ability to thrive in conditions of ambiguity and change; an entrepreneurial spirit; curiosity about diversifying forms of identity and community; facility with social analysis, community organizing, and collaborative problem solving; openness toward emergent forms of spiritual inquiry and practice; multifaith and multicultural inquisitiveness; vigilance toward the holy; and strong doses of humility and fallibilism. With dispositions such as these as our objectives, our education model would need to be deeply experiential and offer to students the space for experimentation.

Our second hypotheses held that we humans are the kind of creatures who *act ourselves into new ways of thinking rather than think ourselves into new ways of acting*. This is related to our first hypothesis insofar as dispositions are settled integrations of intellectual, affective, and moral tendencies formatted by habits and

---

3. Craig Dykstra evokes similar ideas in his excellent essay, "Pastoral and Ecclesial Imagination," in Dorothy Bass and Craig Dykstra, eds., *For Life Abundant*.

4. Our faculty has been strongly influenced by John Dewey's philosophy of education as well as by Paulo Freire's argument against the "banking concept of education" in *Pedagogy of the Oppressed*, and by other critical pedagogy theorists such as Henry Giroux, Peter McLaren, and bell hooks.

practices.⁵ With this in mind we believed our educational model would need to be organized around practices and the formation of habits. This would entail, among other things, designing learning experiences for students that would encourage them to become more critically aware of both their existing learning styles and the cultural paradigms within which they are embedded. As our Professor of Religious Education, Dr. Mark Hicks, likes to point out, this approach to learning often means that students will spend as much time *unlearning* old habits as they will devote to learning new ones: the art of unknowing is at the heart of the art of ministry.

Though our third hypothesis might seem to conflict with the first and second, it actually directly interrelates them. This is the idea that in order to make theological education more financially and geographically accessible to the changing demographics of ministry students, not to mention more relevant to the world, *we would need to develop a low-residency, high-intensity hybrid educational model.* As one of only two Unitarian Universalist denominational seminaries in the United States, it was especially important for us to find a way to make our degree program more accessible to students who live all over North America. The challenge was to do this in a way that supported rather than undermined our commitments to practices and the formation of dispositions.

This challenge, of course, is one that many seminaries and theological educators are currently facing. The dilemma concerns the possibility of creating and sustaining the kind of learning community necessary to ministerial formation in a world in which community is being reconfigured by new forms of interconnection. We seem to be moving toward a post-physical form of

---

5. This hypothesis reflects the influence of pragmatism on our thinking, especially John Dewey's. See especially *Human Nature and Conduct*. We've also been informed by theorists who take up the broader societal significance of practice and habits such as Pierre Bourdieau, Michel Foucault, and Anthony Giddens. We've also been paying increasing attention to new work in the neurosciences which supports the role of practice and action in the shaping of thought patterns. See for example Bruce Wexler's *Brain and Culture: Neurobiology, Ideology, and Social Change* and James E. Zull's *The Art of Changing the Brain*. More generally, our commitment to action and practice is related to the emphasis in liberal religion on orthopraxy over orthodoxy.

community in which the virtual has become the real. Whether or not this is so, it is certainly the case that we are living in a time in which the very idea of community is being relentlessly unformed, reformed, and transformed. We chose to interpret this as an opportunity rather than an impediment. After all, why should it be assumed that a formative learning community must take a particular kind of shape, such as traditional residency on or near a physical campus? Might limiting the contextual form of theological education actually constrict our encounters with the sacred? Why can't or shouldn't the context of theological learning take a variable shape, determinate and bounded at certain times, dissipated and unbounded at others? Might there be spiritual and even pedagogical value in a form of learning that is designed to be experienced as a series of transformations, shape-changes—a form that is perforated, open, and protean, more like the holy, more like the actual world? We believed so.

It became clear to us through our conversations that there were theological shifts embedded within our methodology and pedagogical hypotheses. Foremost among these was the yearning to recover theology as *a religious praxis* from its reduction to a *religious science*.[6] The history of theology's reduction is a long and convoluted one that most readers know well enough. As a result of it, however, one of the long-standing tasks of modern theology has been the apologetic one of articulating and then justifying a place for theology within the modern academy's ordering of disciplines. This is not an unimportant task, but it wasn't ours. Our task was to facilitate among our students a shift from theology viewed as science to theology embodied as a critical expression of religious life.

Getting clear about the importance of theological praxis helped us to identify another theological problem and another important theological shift. Our emerging model both reflected and entailed a critique of the individualist excesses of liberal theology and Unitarian Universalism. One of the theological sources of this individualism is liberal theology's general suspicion of external

---

6. Of course a classic critique of this, which deeply informs us, is Gutierrez, *A Theology of Liberation*.

authorities such as Scripture and tradition. With the suspicion of external authority, liberal theology turned inward to individual experience (reason and conscience) as a primary theological source. But it turns out, of course, that experience is no less opaque or less controverted than tradition and Scripture. The individualist religious culture that is the legacy of liberal theology's experiential turn makes the always difficult work of building and sustaining religious communities even more difficult. Besides this, liberal theology's experiential turn has privileged conceptions of reason and conscience that universalize the particular experiential standpoint of white male privilege.

It is important to say here that Unitarian Universalism's spiritual individualism and liberal theology's theological experientialism, and the social dilemmas they breed, parallel the cultural dynamics and the social contradictions of political progressivism. Political progressivism has for at least three decades been dominated by an expressivist politics of identity. This is no doubt partly why political progressivism is so fragmented socially. It has also made it difficult for the left to articulate a coherent progressive vision and to get organized around it.[7] The importance of this is that within Unitarian Universalism, and within liberal Protestantism more generally, spiritual individualism, theological experientialism, and the politics of identity overlap and intensify one another. They can't really be addressed in isolation from one another. Movement through and beyond these problems could be aided by designing an educational model that shifted the center of liberal theology from individual religious experience to the religious (and political) work of building mutually empowering relationships across difference.

---

7. This is well argued, and provocatively so, by Lisa Duggan in her book *The Twilight of Equality*.

TouchPoint[SM]: An Unapologetically Progressive, Academically Rigorous, and Spiritually Grounded Model of Theological Education

The Meadville Lombard TouchPoint[SM] educational model is much more than an expression of Meadville Lombard's will not to die. It is instead a dynamically charged effort to equip Unitarian Universalist ministers to lead religious communities of justice, equity, and compassion and to vitalize progressive religious engagement with the broader world. It is an approach to theological education built on a praxis model of learning that integrates the theory and practice of ministry through the whole of the curriculum. This contrasts with most other models in theological education, such as our former one, in which classroom learning and field work are staggered. In addition to integrating theory and practice, it offers a hybrid residency format that combines intervals of intensive on-campus classroom learning with independent, small-group, and mentored learning off-campus. This hybrid format makes it possible for students to experience formation within an identity-based seminary while also learning with and from diverse communities and congregational environments closer to their homes. Students no longer need to choose between moving their homes and families to attend a denominational seminary and staying at home and "making do" with whichever seminary is closest to them. Here's how it works.

Students from all over North America, and from other countries such as Japan, India, Azerbaijan, and Norway, come to Chicago to take intensive week-long courses during three to four learning intervals each year—in the fall, during January, in the spring, and in the summer. Rather than discuss each of these in detail, we will focus on the fall and January experiences as representative. The fall interval is structured around cohort learning. Early in September, incoming and returning students meet together with faculty for two days of intensive community building, advising, and some initial classroom work introducing the cohorts to their thematic tracks for the year. Once students return home after the fall convocation, they commence to prepare for their week-long January intensive courses and to participate in the community or congregational internship appropriate to their cohort. The fall work that precedes January intensives is multi-modal. In addition to reading and writing assignments, most courses include practical field work of some kind, periodic conference calls facilitated by faculty, the viewing of films and YouTube videos, and the use of Facebook and Twitter for student-student and student-faculty interaction.

In early January the students return to campus for a two-day learning convocation preceding three consecutive weeks of intensive courses. The whole community participates in the learning convocation: students, faculty, teaching ministers, and other invited guests. During this time we worship together, hear from keynote speakers, dialogue in small groups, and engage in integrative aesthetic exercises (e.g., improvisational theater, found object storytelling). Each year's convocation is organized around a different theme. Past themes have concerned the role of worship in shaping a multicultural congregation, ministry in a time of economic uncertainty, and the diverse cultural images of power that influence ministerial authority. In addition to the intrinsic value of the convocation's content, the experience binds the learning community together and helps students and faculty to integrate the three weeks of intensive courses that follow it.

The experience of January (and summer, and spring) intensives is, well, *intense*. There was a time, not long ago, when we had some misgivings about the possibility of creating and sustaining a learning community without a residential student body. It turns out that these misgivings have been proven wrong. To the contrary, in fact, the high-intensity format of our low-residency model actually deepens community. We call it the "summer camp" effect. During the relatively short time that students are on campus together, they are with each other almost constantly. They take classes together, they cook and share meals, they share rental housing, they attend evening lectures and other functions on campus, and they partake of the richness of Chicago's extracurricular opportunities. While it does take more effort and ingenuity to sustain this communalism once students return to their various home places, this effort only leads us all to be more intentional about the process, which in turn positively feeds back into the learning community. Students stay in touch by phone, email, and social media. And we as a faculty and staff stay in constant contact with them as well, guiding student preparation for intensive classes and advising them by phone, podcast, and social media.

While our model includes courses in theology, history, pastoral care, religious education, and the arts of ministry, the curriculum is anchored by our Signature Courses, a sequence of three year-long, multi-credit, multidisciplinary, multimedia, collaboratively taught internships: Community Studies, Congregational Studies, and Leadership Studies. These courses combine rigorous cohort-based seminar teaching and learning with sustained field educational experiences in community and congregational settings. At the beginning of each Signature Course, the faculty subdivides each cohort into smaller dialogue groups, groups of three to four students who work together in various ways through the year. Learning is organized around weekly assignments. Each student is expected to complete the assignment individually, but then students process their work in their dialogue groups and submit a collectively written summary. There are several pedagogical advantages to this small group structure: it promotes more student interaction, it allows students to learn deeply about one another, and because each student is doing work in a different setting, it provides each student with at least two additional "worlds" (diverse community sites around the country and globe, large and small congregations all through North America) through which to consider their assignments. The faculty provides weekly written feedback to each dialogue group, produces a weekly podcast, and facilitates monthly teleconferences and intensive on-campus workshops twice each year.

In what follows, rather than detailing each Signature Course, we will focus on Community Studies, which we (Welch and Hogue) co-teach. Community Studies is intentionally taught as the first course in the Signature Course sequence. It thereby initiates the process of formation for ministry not only outside of congregations, but even outside of religion altogether. The idea is to shake things up early by providing experiences that unsettle student assumptions and challenge their prejudices, thereby laying the groundwork not only for deeper vocational insight but also for reimagining what church can and should be. Students commit to working eight to ten hours per week in a local community service organization. These have included everything from local hospice programs to animal shelters, from AIDS counseling centers to after school programs, from centers for victims of torture and refugees to homeless shelters, from food kitchens and addictions rehabilitation to immigrant farmer networks and job training facilities. Whatever the community organization happens to be, we expect that it will be staffed by and serve populations with whom the student has little prior experience. In addition, students are expected to take up tasks and work in their community sites in ways that move them out of their comfort zone. For example, though some of our students have considerable community nonprofit leadership experience, they are guided to work on projects that allow them to feel and to see things from a different perspective. As a way to encourage open-mindedness and an entrepreneurial approach to learning, we as a faculty like to reinforce that there is nothing from which we can't learn. There's much to be learned from peeling potatoes with a coworker, for example, about the critical importance of seemingly menial work to the building of community rapport and morale. There's wisdom to be found, almost always, in sharing a meal with coworkers and clients who have experienced the world through the veil of differently colored skin, or class location, or sexual orientation. In these and other ways, students in Community Studies are immersed in defamiliarizing experiences and relationships that generate vital questions about the nature of community engagement, leadership, service, and the vocation of ministry. Complementing these questions and experiences, faculty lead students through diverse assignments that provide students with new ways of seeing and thinking about beauty and suffering, agency and social capital, about the forms and uses of social analysis, identity and difference, about public theology and the changing configurations of the religious and secular, and about the boundaries of the sacred and profane.

Community Studies facilitates intentional encounters between students and diverse populations whose wisdom has been and continues to be marginalized by traditional theological practices. Students learn many lessons through these encounters, the risks they entail, and the courage they demand. Not infrequently, this learning comes through failure and miscommunication. It's good for students, especially students in formation for ministry, to learn how to learn from their mistakes rather than to be derailed by them. Above all, perhaps, students discover in Community Studies how essential empathy, risk-taking, social initiative, and humility are to truly being of service to others. These insights, and the habits they catalyze—such as listening before speaking, building trust and establishing rapport before managing or organizing, taking time to celebrate and to notice and share beauty, doing *with* rather than doing *for*, presuming the presence of wisdom in unexpected places, expecting the unexpected—are critically important to forming the dispositions required of effective ministry in our changing, hurting, glorious world. Community Studies seeks to move students to the critical ministerial insight that *ministry is not about them* (we sometimes refer to the course as "getting over yourself 101") and to the critical theological imperative to reimagine and to activate *new ways of being the church and living religiously*.

Congregational and Leadership Studies are structured in basically the same way as Community Studies—they are team-taught, cohort-based, multidisciplinary, praxis courses that combine independent, small-group, and whole class learning. Differently, however, students in these courses work for up to twenty hours per week in their teaching congregations, transitioning through the two years from the role of observer, to participant, to ministerial leader. In terms of the sequence of the Signature Courses, students can advance to Congregational Studies only after Community

Studies and to Leadership Studies only after Congregational Studies. The intention behind this sequence is for students to move into congregational work with a deepened attunement to the world's diversity and needs and to their own gifts and talents. The pedagogical arc of the Signature Course sequence is designed to form students into Unitarian Universalist ministers who are not only committed to justice, equity, and compassion as ideals, but who also have the capacities and dispositions necessary to undertaking the difficult work of bringing those ideals to reality.

Conclusion

In conclusion, Meadville Lombard's TouchPoint^{SM} model of theological education provides a low-residency, high-intensity educational experience that empowers students to integrate theoretical learning with the realities of professional ministry in a multicultural, religiously diverse, and politically and morally tumultuous world. It provides a laboratory within which students learn to become more *attuned* to the contextual nature of learning and ministry, *aligned* with the values of Unitarian Universalism and the Meadville Lombard mission, *alert* to the strategic roles, tasks, and callings of liberal religious ministry, *aware* of the need for collaboration with communities within and outside Unitarian Universalism, and *attentive* to the complex cultural factors and dynamics that shape human experience and systems. Our institutional self-assessments and student assessments indicate that we are meeting our objectives: students are more satisfied with their seminary education; they appreciate the relevance of praxis learning to ministry in the "real world"; and they are more confidently equipped to work across the various lines of difference that shape our world. External assessments have also been very positive. In August 2013, for example, the ATS reaffirmed a ten-year accreditation for Meadville Lombard and highlighted as some of our "distinctive strengths" our Signature Courses, our commitment to team teaching and service learning, our "integration of praxis and theological reflection in multicultural contexts," and the development of an "agile" educational model "that is mission-driven, market-sensitive, and monetarily sustainable." In these ways the Meadville Lombard TouchPoint℠ model is infusing new life into our school and is seeding the world with a host of new ministers prepared to lead progressive religious communities in the joyful struggle of realizing a more just, equitable, and compassionate world.

Bibliography

Bass, Dorothy, and Craig Dykstra, eds. *For Life Abundant: Practical Theology, Theological Education and Christian Ministry.* Grand Rapids: Eerdmans, 2008.

Dewey, John. *Human Nature and Conduct.* New York: Henry Holt, 1922.

Duggan, Lisa. *The Twilight of Equality: Neoliberalism, Cultural Politics, and the Attack on Democracy.* Boston: Beacon, 2003.

Freire, Paulo. *Pedagogy of the Oppressed.* New York: Continuum, 1970.

Gutierrez, Gustavo. *A Theology of Liberation: History, Politics and Salvation.* Translated and edited by Sister Caridad Inda and John Eagleson. Maryknoll, NY: Orbis, 1973.

Wheeler, Barbara G., et al. "How are We Doing? The Effectiveness of Theological Schools as Measured by The Vocation and Views of Graduates." *Auburn Studies,* December, 2007, 1–31.

Wexler, Bruce. *Brain and Culture: Neurobiology, Ideology, and Social Change.* Cambridge, MA: MIT Press, 2006.

Wind, James P., and David J. Wood. *Becoming a Pastor: Reflections on the Transition into Ministry.* Durham, NC: Alban Institute Special Report, 2008.

Zull, James E. *The Art of Changing the Brain: Enriching the Practice of Teaching by Exploring the Biology of Learning.* Sterling, VA: Stylus, 2002.

6

A Reform Amounting to a Revolution
New York Theological Seminary and Theological Education for the City

Dale T. Irvin

One of the most important insights that the study of World Christianity has taught us over the past several decades is that when it comes to theology, historical location and context matter.[1] Looking forward is always looking forward from a particular historical location and context. What we perceive is interpreted to no small degree through the lenses provided for us by our various historical locations and contexts.[2] Even when our lenses are multiple and we are capable of shifting them to gain different

---

1. For my own fuller understanding of the field of study called "World Christianity," see Irvin, "What is World Christianity?"

2. For an excellent analysis of the role that social and cultural location play in hermeneutics, especially biblical hermeneutics, see Segovia and Tolbert, eds., *Reading from this Place: Vol. 1, Social Location and Biblical Interpretation in the United States* and idem, *Reading from this Place: Vol. 2, Social Location and Biblical Interpretation in Global Perspective*. For more information specifically on how these issues have been incorporated into the curriculum of New York Theological Seminary, see Norman K. Gottwald, "Framing Biblical Interpretation at New York Theological Seminary: A Student Self-Inventory on Biblical Hermeneutics," in *Reading from this Place: Vol. 1*, 251–61.

perspectives, they remain partial, incremental, and incomplete. There is no universal human historical lens that would allow us to see everything all at once this side of eternity. That alone belongs to God, who remains a mystery. Our reading of the mystery is always partial and perspectival.[3]

I begin this chapter accordingly by looking at the future of theological education from a particular institutional location in which my historical perspective has been formed. I have worked in theological education for most of my career in one of the most culturally diverse cities of the world, in a school of theological education that is one of the most diverse in the world. New York Theological Seminary (NYTS) has been my institutional home for more than three decades now. We educate women and men for religious leadership in complex urban contexts. We do it by engaging the city itself in interactive ways that seek to integrate the various aspects of the urban environment (civic organizations, government agencies, community organizations, local businesses, financial institutions, the legal system, state corrections, and faith-based communities and institutions) with the various components of theological learning (Bible, theology, history, ethics, social sciences, and the arts of ministry). Our assumption is that religion is part of the fabric of urban life, and that churches and other religious communities are key components of the urban environment. Engaging the city (not just New York City but the city more generally) is integral to all aspects of life and learning at NYTS because religion is integral to the life of the city.[4]

3. For an excellent analysis that shifts the discussion from "relative" and "relativism" to "perspectival" and "perspectivism" in theology, see Sarah Coakley, *Christ without Absolutes*.

4. Over the past decade NYTS has developed interactive learning using an "action-reflection" method primarily through the Center for the Study and Practice of Urban Religion, previously called the "Ecologies of Learning" project. Employing both quantitative and qualitative academic research tools in courses such as Church and Community Analysis or Critical Interpretation, and through special educational offerings provided to both students and members of faith-based organizations, the Seminary seeks to help urban religious communities and students in programs of theological education work together to better understand the immediate neighborhoods and the wider

Furthermore, because this is New York City, where almost half of the population is now first- or second-generation immigrants, and where one can find children who were born in almost every other nation on earth, by engaging the city NYTS is also engaging the world. We have been self-consciously providing theological education for a global religious community for decades. We have offered entire degree programs at the Doctor of Ministry level in several languages, and have taught classes in the Masters level in several languages as well. It is our experience that urbanization and globalization in the twenty-first center are converging forces, and that urban ministry studies and global mission studies are for all intents and purposes becoming one.[5]

The history of engaging the city in theological education was part of the fabric of NYTS almost from its inception.[6] The Seminary began its institutional life in 1901 as the Bible Teachers College in Montclair, New Jersey. Wilbert Webster White, the founder and first president of the school, located it initially in Montclair because it was the home town of his brother-in-law, John R. Mott. Mott was one of the founding figures of the twentieth-century ecumenical movement, served for many years as the General Secretary of the International YMCA Committee, and played an important if sometimes reluctant role in keeping his brother-in-law's

---

urban context of which their various religious communities are a vital part. For more information on the historical roots of the action-reflection model, see Younger, *From New Creation to Urban Crisis*. On the accomplishments of the earlier "Ecologies of Learning" project that was guided by Lowell Livezey, see Cimino, Mian, and Huang, eds., *Ecologies of Faith in New York City* and Gobin, "Understanding Our Ecologies of Faith."

5. I am aware of the distinction that Lamin Sanneh and others have made between "world" Christianity and "global" Christianity in *Whose Religion is Christianity?* among other places. A more sustained theoretical discussion of the distinction between the worldly and the global can be found in Mignolo, *Local Histories/Global Designs*.

6. For a fuller history of White and Biblical Seminary in New York, see the unpublished monograph by Virginia Brereton, *The History of the Biblical Seminary in New York 1900–1965* (1987), in the NYTS archives in Columbia University.

school running.⁷ White was a graduate of Yale University, where he completed a PhD in Old Testament in 1891 under his mentor William Rainey Harper. White's dissertation, which was titled "The Historical Situation in Isaiah I-XXXIX," made use of the new historical critical method to examine the background for what came to be known as First Isaiah.⁸ After finishing Yale, White assumed a position at Xenia Theological Seminary before leaving in 1894 at the invitation of Dwight L. Moody to become the Associate Director of the Moody Bible Institute in Chicago for two years. He left Moody at the invitation of the YMCA to teach the Bible for two years to missionaries from Europe and North America in India. After leaving India and staying briefly in England, where he was able to raise some funding, White returned to the USA with the goal of founding his own school. His sojourn through theological education had convinced him that none of the various institutional models of his day were adequate for preparing leaders for the world in which they were serving. In a brief outline he typed up in 1936 for a proposed autobiography that he never finished, White wrote that by 1900 he had become "clearly convinced that a reform was needed in theological education amounting practically to a revolution."⁹

At the heart of that revolution was a commitment to studying and teaching the Bible in one's first language free as much as possible from preconceived confessional or ideological commitments. White called it "the inductive Bible method," and it eventually became closely identified with his legacy.¹⁰ But there was another

---

7. Hopkins, *John R. Mott, 1865–1955*, 680, writes that during the Great Depression, "A chronic burden [for Mott] was brother-in-law Will White's Biblical Seminary, which Mott could not bring himself to sustain financially, but with some grumbling did on occasion help to bail out."

8. See *Doctors of Philosophy of Yale University with the Titles of Their Dissertations 1861–1915*, 29. One of the two original copies of White's dissertation is now part of the archives of New York Theological Seminary at Columbia University, a gift from members of his family in 2007.

9. White, "Outline of My Autobiography," 1.

10. See Eberhardt, *The Bible in the Making of a Minister*, and Bauer and Traina, *Inductive Bible Study*, 1–7.

aspect of his legacy that has not been fully appreciated by those who know and appreciate of his contribution to biblical studies. The inductive method always ended with the question of application of the text to the world in which its reading took place. In the *Prospectus* that White published in 1900 announcing the opening of the Bible Teacher's College in Montclair, he noted that students would be expected to spend at least one day each week in ministry in a church in New York City to put their skills in teaching the Bible into practice.[11] The following year he moved the school to New York City in order to provide students more direct opportunities for ministry in its intense urban context. Fifteen years later he would advertise the school as being "Situated in the heart of the great Western Metropolis with all the cosmopolitan advantages incidental to its location" and "Affording also the great cultural advantages of a cosmopolitan company of students, representing (1914–15) twenty-eight denominations, twenty-five countries, thirty states of the Union, and over one hundred and twenty colleges, universities, and seminaries."[12] "It is a Divinity School, evangelical, interdenominational, and intervocational, designed for the training of ministers and other Christian leaders and workers" White explained.[13] As he wrote on another occasion, "We seek to biblicize, and to cosmopolitanize Christian leadership."[14] The notion of an evangelical, cosmopolitan, interdenominational, intervocational school committed to educating ministers, leaders, and workers both of and for the city has deep roots at NYTS.

In 1921 after receiving an absolute charter from New York State, The Bible Teachers Training School became The Biblical Seminary in New York. White continued to guide the school through the 1930s, leading it to go against the grain of Protestant

11. White, *Bible Teachers College Prospectus of First Session*, 14.

12. "The Bible Teachers Training School: A Brief Statement of It's Design, Scope, Organization, Equipment, Curriculum, History and Principles," *The Bible Review* 1, no. 2 (1916), inside front cover.

13. "The Bible Teachers Training School: A Brief Statement of It's Design, Scope, Organization, Equipment, Curriculum, History and Principles," *The Bible Review* 1, no. 2 (1916), inside front cover.

14. White, "The Purpose of The Biblical Seminary in New York," 271.

A Reform Amounting to a Revolution

theological education in North America on a number of counts. First, White sought to steer the seminary clear of either side of the fundamentalist-modernist or conservative-liberal controversy that was engulfing much of Protestant Christianity elsewhere in North America during those decades. White had come from a conservative Presbyterian background, and Biblical Seminary was usually identified as being on the conservative side of the theological spectrum. But White made sure that major figures identified with liberal Protestantism, beginning with his own teacher at Yale, William Rainey Harper, who was tapped by John D. Rockefeller to become the first president of the University of Chicago in 1891, regularly lectured at Biblical Seminary. White never disputed the veracity of historical critical readings of the Bible. He simply did not find them very useful for preparing people for various roles of leadership in the church in the city. The inductive method that White championed rejected any theory, be it of inerrancy and infallibility on one side or historical criticism and evolution on the other, as deductive in nature. The Bible was to be studied and applied free as much as possible of dogmatic impediments. The "biblio-centric" curriculum sought to avoid confessional theological commitments, be they conservative or liberal. White refused on these grounds to allow any statement of biblical inerrancy or infallibility to become part of Biblical Seminary's identity as such statements clearly violated the principle of the inductive method by allowing a doctrinal or confessional conviction to take precedence over the actual reading of the biblical text in its entirely by itself. Biblical Seminary was evangelical without first being fundamentalist.

Free of any binding confessional or dogmatic basis other than its commitment to the Bible, Biblical Seminary would welcome students from a wide range of theological perspectives.[15] White boasted that in the first decade of the school's life there were more than forty denominations represented within its student body. It was also one of the only accredited graduate schools of theological education in North America in the twentieth century not to follow

---

15. See Nolt, "An Evangelical Encounter," 389–417.

the familiar fourfold curriculum of Bible, church history, systematic theology, and practical theology that become normative in the nineteenth century.[16] The Biblical Seminary in New York had no trained systematic theologian on its faculty during its first decades. The faculty were made up of biblical scholars and members of the practical field teaching mission and ministry.[17]

Biblical Seminary was committed to training people for ministry in a cosmopolitan context, specifically that of the "great Western Metropolis" known as New York City. It was also committed to training not just ordained clergy, but leaders and workers of all categories. In this regard White challenged the clerical paradigm that Edward Farley and others have criticized, and which has reigned in theological education among Protestant communities since the Reformation of the sixteenth century.[18] Protestant communions whose churches were under the governance of civil authorities (the so-called Magisterial Reformation) in the sixteenth-century opted mostly for models of theological education that focused on the training of ordained clerics who were permitted by civic authorities to preach in public settings and officiate over the sacraments. In doing so they reasserted hierarchical patterns of clericalism that worked against the democratic tendencies that their movement had unleashed and disempowered the majority of believers, the so-called "laity" in their congregations.

More important for the life of the school, White and others understand what they were doing to be educating religious leaders and not just pastors. By focusing on training candidates to teach the Bible, he was opening the door not just to lay persons, but explicitly to women who made up the majority of the student body. The Biblical Seminary in New York was one of the few schools of graduate theological education that welcomed women into its

---

16. On the fourfold curriculum see Thiemann, "Toward a Critical Theological Education," 1–13; and Thiemann, "Making Theology Central in Theological Education," 106–8.

17. For a reflection upon the impact this curriculum had upon at least one graduate of The Biblical Seminary, see Peterson, *The Pastor*, 15–16 and 84–85.

18. See Farley, *Theologia*.

degree programs. Women were in the majority of the student body during the school's first decades. Graduates included such notable leaders as Nelle Morton and Maria Kim.

Alongside the commitment to lay leadership and women, White brought a strong international perspective to his work in theological education. This perspective was shaped by the contemporary world missionary movement, in which he was so much a part. As noted already, John R. Mott, who was the General Secretary of the International YMCA, one of the key leaders of the Student Christian Movement (after 1895 the World Students' Christian Federation), and the Chair of the Planning Committee for the 1910 World Missionary Conference held in Edinburgh, Scotland, was White's brother-in-law. White was close with many other leaders of the world missionary movement such as Arthur Tappan Pierson, editor of the *Missionary Review of the World*, who also lectured at the Bible Teacher's Training College during its first years. International students were part of the school almost from its inception.

The second generation of leadership at Biblical Seminary in the 1940s focused more intentionally on the inductive Bible method and the bibliocentric curriculum.[19] More emphasis was placed on preparing candidates for ordained ministry, resulting in a decided shift in the make-up of the student body. Men began to outnumber women for the first time. By the 1950s White's legacy concerning the "inductive Bible study" was being eclipsed by the work of his student, Robert A. Traina, whose name continues to be closely associated with the method.[20] The city did not disappear entirely from Biblical Seminary's horizons, as the reflections of Eugene Peterson noted above indicate. It had, however, diminished significantly from view in the life and curriculum of the school.[21]

---

19. See Eberhardt, *The Bible in the Making of Ministers*.

20. See Traina, *Methodical Bible Study*. For a recent assessment of Traina and the enduring value of the method, see Abraham, "Inductive Bible Study, Divine Revelation, and Canon," 6–20.

21. See Brereton, *History of the Biblical Seminary of New York*.

A precipitous drop in enrollment, mounting costs of maintaining the Seminary's building, and external pressures regarding accreditation all came together in the 1960s to bring Biblical Seminary to the edge of closing. In an effort to shed what some in leadership at least perceived to be the impression that the Seminary's name indicated it was a Bible school and not a graduate school of theological education, the trustees voted to change it in 1965 to New York Theological Seminary. Four years later they called George W. "Bill" Webber to be its president. Under Webber's leadership NYTS opened a new era not just in its own institutional history, but in the history of theological education more generally in North America.

For many, the decision to call Webber to be the president of NYTS seemed to represent a radical departure from the seminary's history. Webber had earlier served as the Dean of Students at Union Theological Seminary in New York and was still an adjunct faculty member there. That alone was sufficient for some to perceive him as being theologically liberal. His predecessor as president of NYTS, John Sutherland Bonnell, who was the Senior Pastor Emeritus of Fifth Avenue Presbyterian Church in Manhattan, was cited in an article published in the *New York Times* as fearing that Webber's appointment would lead to an "overemphasis of social-action objectives at the expense of evangelism."[22]

Union was only part of Webber's background prior to being called to become president of NYTS, however. Two decades earlier along with several other graduates of Union Theological Seminary he had moved into East Harlem, at the time one of the poorest neighborhoods in New York City, to launch an ecumenical ministry that brought together evangelism, community organizing, social action, and public advocacy. They called the project the East Harlem Protestant Parish as they operated as a cooperative ministerial leadership team.[23] Their initial bases in the community were congregations that were part of what was then called ecumenical

22. Dugan, "Seminary to Turn From Academic to Urban Work," 34.

23. On the history of the East Harlem Protestant Parish, see Kenrick, *Come Out the Wilderness*; and Webber, *The East Harlem Protestant Parish*.

Protestantism, or what became known as mainline Protestantism.[24] They came with theological degrees from Union, Yale, or Harvard as members of "middle class" Protestant churches in America who were seeking to evangelize their own churches as much as the poor among whom they worked. To this end they sought to build alliances with members of the neighborhood, many of whom were from Spanish-speaking Pentecostal Churches that had taken root in East Harlem.[25]

East Harlem Protestant Parish had an enormous impact around the world in reinvigorating urban ministry that was especially concerned with serving the poor.[26] Community programs that it helped spawn in the immediate neighborhood included an after-school tutoring center, drug rehabilitation programs, a job placement center, several affordable housing projects, and a neighborhood credit union. Several new congregations emerged as part of their efforts as well. One of the underlying commitments that guided the Parish was a perceived need for new structures of accountability for ministry. The instruction found in Jeremiah 29:7 "to seek the *shalom* of the city" was one of their guiding scriptural principals in this regard. The marks of faithfulness in the city were not necessarily the same as the traditional marks of faithfulness within the church, they discovered.[27]

---

24. The other two founding leaders of the project were Donald L. Benedict, and J. Archie Hargraves. They were soon joined by Norman Eddy, Peggy Eddy, Helen Archibald, George Todd, Cathy Todd, George Calvert, Elizabeth Calvert, and Letty Russell among others, all of whom left a published legacy to document their work.

25. The next generation of leaders in theological education that came from the EHPP effort included names like Ray Rivera, Samuel Solivan, Robert W. Pazmiño, and Benjamin Alicea-Lugo.

26. Younger, *From New Creation to Urban Crisis*, 31, writes, "The history of urban mission in the period following World War II begins with the formation of the East Harlem Protestant Parish in New York City in 1948."

27. This is not to say that East Harlem Protestant Parish along with other urban ministry projects of its era were without severe shortcomings. Benjamin Alicea-Lugo's dissertation, which was completed at Union Seminary in 1989, summarized the project succinctly in the view of some. The title of his work was "Christian Urban Colonizers: A History of the East Harlem Protestant

In 1964 Webber left East Harlem Protestant Parish to launch and direct a national educational program called Metropolitan Urban Service Training (MUST).[28] MUST offered seminary students and graduates from across North America, both clergy and laity, a year-long internship in urban ministry in the New York area in which they were placed in local churches, lived in the neighborhoods where they served, and engaged in intensive reflection on the social, political, cultural, and theological dimensions of their experience. MUST rented office space in Biblical Seminary's building in Manhattan, and in 1967 began collaborating with newly renamed NYTS to offer a one-year STM degree in Urban Ministry that combined its internship program with NYTS courses, some of which were taught by Webber and others involved in leadership in the East Harlem Protestant Parish. When the trustees of NYTS went looking for a new president, they only had to go down a few flights of stairs to knock on Webber's office door.

Webber brought much of the MUST experience and curriculum to NYTS after 1969 as he began to revitalize the seminary's academic mission and programs. But instead of focusing

---

Parish in New York City, 1948–68." What one might now call Alicea's "postcolonial" critique is an important corrective to missional theologies that fail to grasp the changed conditions of the post-modern and post-colonial global urban context. On the relationship between colonial and postcolonial theoretical discourses, see Loomba, *Colonialism/Postcolonialism*. Interestingly, Webber himself had originally used the language of "God's colony" to describe what he and his other white/Anglo colleagues where doing in East Harlem, which was mostly Black and Latino in the 1950s and 1960s. Webber changed the trope significantly in his later work to talk about "a community of exiles and pilgrims." See Webber, *God's Colony in Man's World*; and then Webber, *Today's Church*.

28. Funded initially by the Methodist Church, MUST was originally an acronym for Methodist Urban Service Training, but after its first year Webber and others who were involved in leadership, including Randolph Nugent, who was later to serve as the Director of MUST, become becoming General Secretary of the Board of Global Missions for what after 1968 became the United Methodist Church, decided it needed to broaden its ecumenical focus and thus changed "Methodist" to "Metropolitan," thereby accounting for the obvious redundancy in the name. On the history of MUST, see Younger, *From New Creation to Urban Crisis*; and Dunn, *New Ministries for the City at Metropolitan Urban Service Training, New York City*.

A Reform Amounting to a Revolution

upon preparing seminarians and clergy from mainline Protestant churches for ministry in the city, he reversed polarities and began to focus upon clergy and lay leaders who were serving in urban congregations in poor neighborhoods in the city, but who were also often without accredited theological education. After one year he suspended the Master of Divinity (MDiv) degree program and opened several non-accredited Certificate programs that were both open and attractive to newer constituencies. The goal was to provide urban church leaders, both lay and ordained, who did not hold a Bachelor's degree with access to the resources of theological education beyond those that were being offered by the more traditional Bible institutes in which many urban leaders were being trained. After several years the seminary began to offer accredited degree programs again but now in formats that were accessible to working urban religious leaders, and with various curricula that were relevant to their context.

In one sense Webber rebuilt NYTS from the ground up. But in another he simply moved forward the initial vision of urban immersion that characterized NYTS from its founding, whose history and place in theological education he was already familiar with when he became president.[29] His intention was to transform the full theological curriculum in a direction that began with the needs of the city, and held itself accountable to the city.[30] Webber often noted that the inspiration for much of his thinking on these issues and for much of his work in urban ministry in general came from his the Dutch missiologist, Johannes C. "Hans" Hoekendijk.[31]

---

29. See Pazmiño, *The Seminary in the City*, and Webber, *Led by the Spirit*. On page 9 Webber writes, "The Auburn History of Theological Education in the United States makes it clear that the founding and early years of the Biblical Seminary marked the only enduring variant to the four-fold curricular pattern that had become normative with the founding of Andover Seminary."

30. See Webber, "The Struggle for Integrity," 3–21.

31. In his earlier writings Webber did not cite Hoekendijk, but in "The Struggle for Integrity," in which he looked back at his years of urban ministry and theological education, he named Hoekendijk several times, quoting him without reference. Writing of the East Harlem Protestant Parish in *Led by the Spirit*, Webber noted: "From the [World Council of Churches] study secretary, Hans Hoekendijk, came the definition of evangelism as involving *kerygma*,

Hoekendijk served as Professor of Mission at Union from 1965 until his death in 1975. Not insignificantly he was the doctoral advisor for another pastor from the East Harlem Protestant Parish, Letty M. Russell, whose 1969 dissertation Hoekendijk directed. Webber was the second member of her dissertation committee.[32]

Hoekendijk, Webber, and Russell had first worked together in the World Council of Churches' Faith and Order study project on the missionary structure of the congregation that emerged from the 1961 New Delhi Assembly.[33] Webber finished his doctoral dissertation at Union Seminary in 1963 while taking part in the study project. The title of his dissertation, "The Missionary Structures of the Congregation: A Study of the Emerging Pattern of Congregational Life Based on the Experience of Protestantism in the Inner City," indicates the degree to which he applied the concept of missional thinking to urban ministry.[34] The argument that they were advancing is that mission is not what the church does in the world. Mission is what the church is.[35] The word *mission* is another way of

---

koinonia, and *diakonia*" (3). In a recent conversation, Dr. William Weisenbach, who was a student at the Seminary in 1968–1969 and later became Vice President, told me that Hoekendijk and Webber joined Letty Russell in teaching the course in the NYTS curriculum that was offered under her name that year.

32. Russell, "Tradition as Mission." The third member of the committee, according to Union's records, was Robert W. Lynn. I thank Millie Ehrlich of Union Seminary for her assistance in confirming these details in Union's archives.

33. The final report of this study project was published as *The Church for Others: Two Reports on the Missionary Structure of the Congregation* (Geneva: World Council of Churches, 1967).

34. Insights from the dissertation were included in a book Webber published in 1964 that was drawn from a number of lectures he had delivered on the experience around the nation, including at Fuller Theological Seminary. See Webber, *The Congregation in Mission.*

35. The words of Emil Brunner are often quoted in this regard: "Mission work does not arise from any arrogance in the Christian Church; mission is its cause and its life. The Church exists by mission, just as a fire exists by burning. Where there is no mission, there is no Church; and where there is neither Church nor mission, there is no faith. It is a secondary question whether by that we mean Foreign Missions, or simply the preaching of the Gospel in the home church. Mission, Gospel preaching, is the spreading out of the fire which

A Reform Amounting to a Revolution

naming the nature of the Christian church, while the term *church* is another way of naming the nature of the Christian mission.[36] As Hoekendijk argued, "That which cannot serve as 'order of missions' has no right to exist as order of the church."[37]

Hoekendijk's missional theology was grounded in a rigorous critique of Western Christendom. He rejected the manner in which church and mission had been separated even in ecumenical theology. He was especially critical of the theological distinction that was often made in Western thinking between "foreign missions" and "homeland missions," or between evangelism and mission. He viewed these as being ideological remnants of Western Christendom. For Hoekendijk both mission and church needed to be turned inside out in a post-Christendom context. The church always found its life beyond its own structures and existence. This was why he argued that church planting and conversion of the nations (*plantatio ecclesiae et conversio gentium*) as had been formulated in the Christendom-mentality of the West in and of themselves could not be the goal of mission.[38] To say that the church is apostolic, he argued, is to say, it is sent, never settled. "Consequently it cannot be firmly established but will always remain *paroikia*, a temporary settlement which can never become a permanent home."[39]

The orders of the church were thus always properly directed beyond the church itself. Through its various ministries of word, sacrament, and service the church was to be showing forth to the world signs of the coming reign of God on earth. Mission in this

---

Christ has thrown upon the earth." Brunner, *The Word and the World*, 108.

36. Stephen Neill argued against this missional definition of the church in *Creative Tension*, where he wrote, "If everything is mission, then nothing is mission" (81). But then one would have to say the same about Colossians 3:11, that if Christ is all and in all, then Christ is nothing.

37. Hoekendijk, *The Church Inside Out*, 159.

38. See "The Church in the Missionary Thinking," 336, where he challenges explicitly the notion of *plantatio ecclesiae* as the goal of mission, a notion that he says derives from the seventeenth century theologian Voetius, the "father" of Protestant missiology.

39. Hoekendijk, "The Church in the Missionary Thinking," 334.

context entailed transformation not just of the world, but of the church in its theology and structures, brought about through fresh encounters with new cultural and historical situations that the church encountered in the world. The world outside the church was the place where the coming reign of God would appear, not in the church itself. According to the New Testament, Hoekendijk argued, the arena of divine salvation or redemption was always the whole world, the *oikumene*. As he put it, "God intends the redemption of the whole of creation."[40] The church was called to be an agent that participated in this work of redemption that God had undertaken in the world. He therefore rejected what he called "church-ism" or "church-centric" theology. The Word of God by which the church lived called it to give itself away in ministry and mission in the world. The church would only find itself, its identity, by joining God and others in the world in the wider project of transformation. Ultimately Christians were called to seek the *shalom* or well-being not of their churches, but of the world into which God had sent them.[41] It was by way of Hoekendijk that Webber and others who followed him in the programs and theologies of urban ministry arrived at the compelling injunction of Jeremiah 7:29, to seek the *shalom* of the city.

The phrase that came to be associated with this theological argument especially among its critics was "the world sets the agenda for the church."[42] The phrase gained wider currency through its association with the 1968 Uppsala Assembly of the World Council of Church.[43] Where it appears in the 1967 report of the World Council study project, *The Church for Others: Two Reports on the Missionary Structure of the Congregation*, it is immediately followed by a reference to the challenge that the civil rights movement was posing to Protestant churches in the USA. It was not the sinful structures of the world that set the agenda for

---

40. Hoekendijk, *The Church Inside Out*, 22.

41. Hoekendijk, "The Church in the Missionary Thinking," 334.

42. See for instance Neuhaus, *The Naked Public Square*, 218, or Ott et al., *Encountering Theology of Mission*, 129–30.

43. See Goodall, *The Uppsala Report 1968*, xviii.

the church. Rather, it was the work of redemption that was taking place in history but that would only find its eschatological fullness in the messianic reign. The positive value assigned to the world was thoroughly eschatological in character. As Hoekendijk put it:

> The exalted Lord, who in and through his own coming has brought the Kingdom 'at hand,' has also opened the doors to the world. The 'world' as correlate of the 'Kingdom' is a Messianic concept. The ends of the earth and the end of time belong together. Eschatology and universality are both dimensions of the Messianic fullness.[44]

It was left to Letty Russell, the third member of the World Council study project who was associated with East Harlem Protestant Parish, MUST, and for a brief time NYTS, to draw the implications of these arguments specifically for theological education. Russell's dissertation, which was completed at Union Seminary in 1967 under Hoekendijk's direction, was titled "Tradition as Mission: Study of a New Current in Theology and Its Implications for Theological Education." One of its most compelling insights concerning both church and theological education clearly reflected the experience of educating in the city.

> [M]inistry as it has been developed in the Christendom situation is becoming more and more dysfunctional in the post-modern world. . . . Unilateral, one track WASP education is becoming dysfunctional in a church which takes its calling to service of the *oikoumene* without any seriousness.[45]

---

44. Hoekendijk, *The Church Inside Out*, 33.

45. Russell, "Tradition as Mission," 315–16 (emphasis original). Interestingly, the quote from page 316 continues, "In this respect much can be learned from Pentecostal groups and from the evangelical Bible colleges about alternative forms of theological education." See also Russell, *Christian Education in Mission*, where she writes, "This book is written in light of fourteen years' experience as teacher and pastor in the East Harlem Protestant Parish. Although it is *not* a description of life in East Harlem, or even of Christian education in the inner city, it is a product of theological reflection in this context" (10).

Looking back on her work several decades later, Russell noted that by the early 1970s she had shifted in theological terminology from "mission" to "liberation," in part to make clearer the implications of her earlier work in mission theology. "I think of God's Mission or action in the world as equivalent to God's liberating action or liberation," she wrote in this regard.[46] The intentional shift in the direction in her theological thinking from "God-church-world" to "God-world-church" resulted in a corresponding "shift from an *ecclesiocentric* to *theocentric* and, for some, to an *oikocentric* perspective."[47]

By the 1980s NYTS had made this same shift in redefining mission as liberation. In the process its programs shifted from being missional to liberational. Field-based and inductive learning in the form of the "action-reflection model" continued to be a part of the Seminary's teaching and learning, but texts such as Paulo Freire's *Pedagogy of the Oppressed* became important components of the curriculum.[48] The Seminary resumed offering the MDiv degree in 1984, but continued to offer certificate programs intended especially for those without a traditional undergraduate degree.[49] The commitment to providing theological education to so-called "non-traditional students," usually defined as working adults,[50] was extended to mean those who have been socially minoritized

---

46. Russell, *Church in the Round*, 90.

47. Russell, *Church in the Round*, 88–89.

48. Email from Keith A. Russell on 5/30/2017. Russell became president following Webber in 1982.

49. Such programs are written into the Seminary's By-Laws today. Article I.3 reads: "Complementary to its graduate programs and cognizant of its responsibility to the various sectors of the Christian community, the Seminary shall also create and provide to clergy and laity non-degree educational opportunities geared to enhance their capability in a diversity of Christian ministries."

50. On the contested definition of a "non-traditional student" see the National Center for Educational Statistics web page at https://nces.ed.gov/pubs/web/97578e.asp,; and Needham Yancey Gulley, "The Myth of the Nontraditional Student," in *Inside Higher Ed* (August 5, 2016), online at https://www.insidehighered.com/views/2016/08/05/defining-students-non traditional-inaccurate-and-damaging-essay.

on the basis of race, class, ethnicity, gender, or sexual orientation. Theological diversity grew as well, resulting in a student body whose members continue to range from identifying themselves as being very conservative to being liberal, progressive, or radical.

Over the past several decades NYTS has continued to pursue theological education that is self-consciously *urbancentric*. The horizons of theological education at NYTS have been the city with all of its complexities, encompassing the churches of the city without being bound or confined by them. The city sets the agenda in this sense. But it is not the neo-liberal city with its inequities of extreme wealth and poverty, or the neo-colonial city that re-inscribes policies of containment and exclusion under the banner of a free market economy that calls us forward.[51] It is instead the just city, resurrection city, or the city that is prefigured in the eschatological vision of a New Jerusalem.[52] These two visions of the city are not unrelated. Theological education seeks to participate in the transformation of the former in the direction of the latter.

A direct corollary of this last point is that theological education needs to seek to train leaders and not managers. At first glance this may seem to be axiomatic in that clergy and other religious professionals are considered by definition to be leaders of their communities. However this is not truly the case. Too often theological education, driven by the perceived need to serve the status quo of existing churches and denominations rather than the wider world around it, has found its purpose in preparing managers and therapists for these congregations.[53] Religious leaders do need managerial skills, but these must be employed in ways that lead communities of faith in ways that empower them to experience transformation.

As it does so, theological education needs to be concerned for the whole city, including all of its inhabitants and the multiple

---

51. See Hackworth, *The Neoliberal City*; and King, *Writing the Global City*.

52. Fainstein, *The Just City*; Soja, *Seeking Spatial Justice*; and Heltzel, *Resurrection City*.

53. See Hough, Jr. and Cobb, Jr., *Christian Identity and Theological Education*, and Hough, Jr. and Wheeler, eds., *Beyond Clericalism*.

ecologies that make it up. Theological education should not be concerned only about training professional clerics, but should seek to energize and educate people more generally to prepare them for religious ministry and service in the world in which they live. Short-term certificate programs and field-based learning are especially important for these purposes. The traditional library is not abandoned in this process as a major resource for teaching and learning; rather the library itself is understood to be a field site, situated in relation to the larger urban context of knowledge. New forms of theological education that are carried out in partnership with other professional bodies and associations in the city are also important, as is the production of sound resources that address specific needs.[54]

Theological education needs to become more clearly incarnated in the urban context, and more critical of the growing economic disparity that is a product of neo-liberal urban policies. Gentrification is a major factor reshaping North American cities in these first decades of the twenty-first century. A considerable portion of what passes for urban ministry and urban theology is little more than church-planting that follows the displacement brought about by gentrification. Such efforts often resemble the missiological theories that accompanied Western colonialism in the nineteenth century, resulting in churches that are *in* the city but not *of* the city.[55] Theological education needs to pay attention to whether it is preparing missionaries from outside the city who plan to come in and save it, or preparing organic leaders who are

---

54. In 2016 NYTS worked closely with the New York State Office for the Prevention of Domestic Violence and the Governor's Office of Faith Based Community Development Services to produce "Domestic Violence and Faith Communities: Guidelines for Leaders," available online at http://www.opdv.ny.gov/professionals/faith/guidelines.pdf.

55. My usage here follows Aloysious Pieris, SJ, Asian Theology of Liberation, where he argues that it is an immediate task of churches *in* Asia to become churches *of* Asia. He observes, "a local church *in* Asia is usually a rich church working *for* the poor, whereas the local church *of* Asia could only be a poor church working *with* the poor, a church that has been evangelized, a church that has become good news to Asians" (36).

A Reform Amounting to a Revolution

already there.[56] It also needs to determine whether or not it is committed to working with, and not for, the urban poor.[57]

Accredited degree programs remain important for theological education in no small part because of the educational form of cultural capital that they generate.[58] Non-accredited programs can offer comparable educational experiences, but having an earned accredited degree carries significant social and cultural advantages in the contemporary urban context. The shift in urban economies over the past several decades in North America from manufacturing to service and finance industries has increased the demand for professional education. One of the results has been to put pressure on pastors of churches and other religious leaders in urban areas, many of whom are without an accredited degree, to earn one. Innovative degree programs that are designed to make such accredited education accessible to those who have been historically shut out of formal educational systems are especially important in this regard.

One of the key examples along these lines has been the accredited Masters of Professional Studies (MPS) degree that NYTS has offered inside Sing Sing Correctional Facility for the past thirty-five years. This degree is open to men throughout the New York State correctional system who are currently incarcerated, who have earned an undergraduate degree, and who have a faith commitment (including a commitment to serving their fellow human beings).[59] Over 500 have now graduated from the

---

56. My concept here of organic leaders follows Antonio Gramsci's notion of organic intellectuals. See Gramsci, *Selections from the Prison Notebooks*, 4–7.

57. See The Advisory Committee on Social Witness Policy of the General Assembly Mission Council/Presbyterian Mission Agency of the Presbyterian Church (USA), *The Gospel from Detroit*.

58. Bourdieu, *Distinction*, 80–82; and Bourdieu, "The Forms of Capital," 241–58.

59. Because New York State prisons are strictly gender-segregated, only men who are incarcerated in a New York State facility can apply for the program in Sing Sing. The lower number of women overall who are incarcerated in New York State, and who hold an undergraduate degree, has prevented the Seminary from offering a similar program for women.

MPS program. They serve as peer counselors, chaplains' assistants, educators, and program leaders inside correctional facilities throughout New York State. Upon release many have gone on to work in non-profit leadership; serve as pastors, imams, and chaplains; teach at the university level; and serve on non-profit boards or government commissions, among other accomplishments. This is but one example of the way a program in theological education can be directed toward specific sectors of the urban context that have been historically marginalized or ignored and play a part in transforming the world.

Finally, theological education needs to take seriously the religious and spiritual pluralism of the city. Theological schools in North America over the past five decades have gone a long way toward becoming more open to other expressions of Christian faith and tradition. Even schools that are identified with particular denomination, church, or communion have not only shown considerable openness to learning from other Christian traditions, but are increasingly learning to welcome others into their institutions. This has not been the case for the most part for what are deemed to be "other religions." Apart from the occasional "interfaith" educational program, theological education in North America remains almost by definition a Christian enterprise. The result has been something of a firewall preventing Christian schools of theological education from taking on the task of educating leaders for other religious communities in the city.

The problem is that such firewalls are increasingly breaking down in everyday life in the city, and in the activities in which religious leaders are engaged. It is a rare church, synagogue, mosque, or temple that does not have members or participants with family members from other religious faith traditions. Chaplaincy as a profession in North America has become thoroughly interfaith and multifaith in character. Even the most conservative pastors and other church leaders are being called upon to pray at civic events or participate in multifaith dialogues and forums. A number of theological schools, such as Hartford Theological Seminary in Hartford, Connecticut, have taken up the challenge to educate leaders of other religious traditions in ways that advance their religious communities. NYTS has been educating African American Muslim leaders for the past thirty-five years. Their numbers have never been large, but their contributions to the NYTS community have been significant. More recently the Seminary's multifaith collaborations have extended to include work with the New York Zen Center for Contemplative Care to offer a Buddhist track in the Master of Arts in Pastoral Care and Counseling, and whose Director supervisors the NYTS program in Clinical Pastoral Education. NYTS also collaborates with the ALEPH Alliance for Jewish Renewal, One Spirit Learning Alliance, and other such partners, extending theological education in new directions among various religious communities in the city. It is more than a matter of showing hospitality to neighbors, although it is this. It is also a matter of working together for the common good to seek the *shalom* of the city afresh.

The city itself is the guide in these efforts. The diversity of its neighborhoods, ethnic communities, and religious traditions calls for increased sensitivities and commitments to true diversity not just in cultural identities but at the deepest theological level. One size cannot fit all in providing theological education for the city. On the other hand, a profound realization that religion is an integral part of the life of the city, and that the city is historically and even ontologically religious and spiritual by nature, provides a unifying vision. Theological education in the city in this regard is a project of reform amounting to a revolution.

Bibliography

Abraham, William J. "Inductive Bible Study, Divine Revelation, and Canon." *The Journal of Inductive Biblical Studies* 1, no. 1 (2014) 6–20.

The Advisory Committee on Social Witness Policy of the General Assembly Mission Council/Presbyterian Mission Agency of the Presbyterian Church (USA). *The Gospel from Detroit: Renewing the Church's Urban Vision*. Louisville: The Office of the General Assembly, Presbyterian Church (USA), 2014.

Bauer, David R., and Robert A. Traina. *Inductive Bible Study: A Comprehensive Guide to the Practice of Hermeneutics*. Grand Rapids: Baker Academic, 2014.

Bourdieu, Pierre. *Distinction: A Social Critique of the Judgement of Taste*. Cambridge, MA: Harvard University Press, 1987.

———. "The Forms of Capital." In *Handbook of Theory and Research for the Sociology of Capital*, edited by John G. Richardson, 241–58. New York: Greenwood, 1986.

Brereton, Virginia Lieson. *History of the Biblical Seminary of New York: 1900–1965*. Unpublished manuscript, Columbia: Burke Library Archives, 1987.

Brunner, Emil. *The Word and the World*. New York: Charles Scribner's Sons, 1931.

Cimino, Richard, Nadia A. Mian, and Weishan Huang, eds. *Ecologies of Faith in New York City: The Evolution of Religious Institutions*. Bloomington, IN: Indiana University Press, 2012.

Coakley, Sarah. *Christ without Absolutes: A Study of the Christology of Ernst Troeltsch*. Rev. ed. London: Clarendon, 1995.

Doctors of Philosophy of Yale University with the Titles of Their Dissertations 1861–1915: Prepared by the Graduate School. New Haven, CT: Yale University, 1916.

Dugan, George. "Seminary to Turn From Academic to Urban Work." *New York Times*, July 6, 1970.

Dunn, Larry Edward. *New Ministries for the City at Metropolitan Urban Service Training, New York City*. Lexington, KY: Lexington Theological Seminary, 1968.

Eberhardt, Charles Richard. *The Bible in the Making of a Minister: The Theological Basis of Theological Education: The Lifework of Wilbert Webster White*. New York: Associate, 1949.

Fainstein, Susan S. *The Just City*. Ithaca, NY: Cornell University Press, 2010.

Farley, Edward. *Theologia: The Fragmentation and Unity of Theological Education*. Minneapolis: Augsburg, 1994.

Gobin, Shirvahna. "Understanding Our Ecologies of Faith: The Ecologies of Learning Project." *CrossCurrents* 58, no. 3 (Fall 2008) 420–25.

Goodall, Norman. *The Uppsala Report 1968: Official Report of the Fourth Assembly of the World Council of Churches, Uppsala July 4–20, 1968*. Geneva: World Council of Churches, 1968.

Gramsci, Antonio. *Selections from the Prison Notebooks*. Translated and edited by Quinton Hoare and Geoffrey Nowell Smith. New York: International, 1971.

Hackworth, Jason R. *The Neoliberal City: Governance, Ideology, and Development in American Urbanism*. Ithaca: Cornell University Press, 2007.

Heltzel, Peter G. *Resurrection City: A Theology of Improvisation*. Grand Rapids: Eerdmans, 2012.

Hoekendijk, Johannes C. *The Church Inside Out*. Philadelphia: Westminster, 1964.

———. "The Church in the Missionary Thinking." *International Review of Missions* 61, no. 2 (1952) 334.

Hoekendijk, Johannes C., William Webber, and Letty M. Russell. *The Church for Others: Two Reports on the Missionary Structure of the Congregation*. Geneva: World Council of Churches, 1967.

Hopkins, C. Howard. *John R. Mott, 1865–1955: A Biography*. Grand Rapids: Eerdmans, 1979.

Hough, Joseph C., Jr., and John B. Cobb, Jr. *Christian Identity and Theological Education*. Atlanta: Scholars, 1985.

Hough, Joseph C., Jr., and Barbara G. Wheeler, eds. *Beyond Clericalism: The Congregation as a Focus for Theological Education*. Atlanta: Scholars, 1988.

Irvin, Dale T. "What is World Christianity?" In *World Christianity: Perspectives and Insights: Essays in Honor of Peter C. Phan*, edited by Jonathan Y. Tan and Anh Q. Tran, 3–26. Maryknoll, NY: Orbis, 2016.

Kenrick, Bruce. *Come Out the Wilderness, The Story of East Harlem Protestant Parish*. New York: Harper and Brothers, 1962.

King, Anthony D. *Writing the Global City: Globalisation, Postcolonialism and the Urban (Architext)*. New York: Routledge, 2016.

Loomba, Ania. *Colonialism/Postcolonialism*. London: Routledge, 1998.

Mignolo, Walter D. *Local Histories/Global Designs: Coloniality, Subaltern Knowledges and Border Thinking*. Princeton, NJ: Princeton University Press, 1999.

Moody-Shepherd, Eleanor. *The Inductive Method: Interpretation of the Bible for the Twentieth Century*. New York Theological Seminary 1, no. 2 (2001).

Neill, Stephen. *Creative Tension*. London: Edinburgh House, 1959.

Neuhaus, Richard John. *The Naked Public Square: Religion and Democracy in America*. Grand Rapids: Eerdmans, 1984.

Nolt, Steven M. "An Evangelical Encounter: Mennonites and the Biblical Seminary in New York." *The Mennonite Quarterly Review* 70, no. 3 (1996) 389–417.

Ott, Craig, et al. *Encountering Theology of Mission: Biblical Foundations, Historical Developments, and Contemporary Issues*. Grand Rapids: Baker, 2010.

Pazmiño, Robert W. *The Seminary in the City: A Study of New York Theological Seminary*. Lanham, MD: University Press of America, 1988.

Peterson, Eugene H. *The Pastor: A Memoir*. New York: HarperOne, 2012.

Russell, Letty M. *Christian Education in Mission*. Philadelphia: Westminster, 1967.

———. *Church in the Round: Feminist Interpretation of the Church*. Louisville: Westminster, 1993.

———. "Tradition as Mission: Study of a New Current in Theology and Its Implications for Theological Education." PhD Dissertation, Union Theological Seminary in New York, 1969.

Sanneh, Lamin. *Whose Religion is Christianity? The Gospel Beyond the West*. Grand Rapids: Eerdmans, 2003.

Segovia, Fernando F., and Mary Ann Tolbert, eds. *Reading from this Place: Vol. 1, Social Location and Biblical Interpretation in the United States*. Minneapolis: Fortress, 1995.

———. *Reading from this Place: Vol. 2, Social Location and Biblical Interpretation in Global Perspective*. Minneapolis: Fortress, 2000.

Soja, Edward W. *Seeking Spatial Justice*. Minneapolis: University of Minnesota Press, 2010.

"The Bible Teachers Training School: A Brief Statement of It's Design, Scope, Organization, Equipment, Curriculum, History and Principles." *The Bible Review* 1, no. 2 (1916) inside front cover.

Thiemann, Ronald F. "Toward a Critical Theological Education." *The Harvard Theological Review* 80, no. 1 (1987) 1–13.

———. "Making Theology Central in Theological Education." *Christian Century* (1987) 106–8.

Traina, Robert A. *Methodical Bible Study: A New Approach to Hermeneutics*. New York: Ganis & Harris, 1952.

Webber, George W. *God's Colony in Man's World*. Nashville: Abingdon, 1960.

———. *Led by the Spirit: The Story of New York Theological Seminary*. New York: Pilgrim, 1990.

———. *The East Harlem Protestant Parish: Study Papers for the MSM Regional Leadership Training Conferences*. Edited by Thomas C. Oden. Nashville: Board of Education of the Methodist Church, 1962.

———. *The Congregation in Mission: Emerging Structures for the Church in an Urban Society*. Nashville: Abingdon, 1964.

———. "The Struggle for Integrity." *Review of Religious Research* 23, no. 1 (1981) 3–21.

———. *Today's Church: A Community of Exiles and Pilgrims*. Nashville: Abingdon, 1979.

White, Wilbert Webster. *Bible Teachers College Prospectus of First Session to be Conducted in Montclair, New Jersey, January until May, 1901*. Montclair, NJ: np, 1900.

White, Wilbert Webster. "Outline of My Autobiography." Unpublished Notes, 1936.

———. "The Purpose of The Biblical Seminary in New York." *Christian Education* 11, no. 4 (1927) 271.

Younger, George D. *From New Creation to Urban Crisis: A History of Action Training Ministries, 1962–1975*. Chicago: Center for the Scientific Study of Religion, 1987.

7

The Change We Need
Race and Ethnicity in Theological Education[1]

WILLIE JAMES JENNINGS

Introduction

LOOK AT THE PHOTOS. You can see the change in those yearly pictures. The bodies of racial and ethnic minorities and women now more heavily sprinkle the formerly monochromatic images of a graduating class and a learned faculty both formerly comprised primarily and often exclusively of serious-looking white men. Fifty years is a long time in the life of an institution, but theological institutions count time slowly where recent (as in an idea, or a scholarly work, or an argument) can mean anywhere from twenty to 200 years. So this change in the bodies that inhabit theological institution is truly a recent change and a painfully slow one for many institutions. The invasion of predominately white theological institutions by racial and ethnic minorities is one of the single most important changes in theological education in the latter half

1. Originally published in *Theological Education* 49.1 (2014) 35–42.

of the twentieth century and the beginning of the twenty-first century. That change has had a profound effect on the ecologies of institutions, placing a new set of dynamics in the midst of 1) academic theological conversation, 2) the teaching life in the theological academy, and 3) the formation process of students.

New Interlocutors in Old Conversations/Old Interlocutors in New Conversations

Theological education is not a new thing for people of color, especially in the United States. For example, theological education has been going on in historical black institutions since before the turn of the last century, and there have been formally trained black and brown Christian intellectuals from the very beginning of the colonial moment. What constitutes the new in the last fifty years is the unanticipated presence of racial and ethnic minorities in places both spatial and conceptual where their voices had not been imagined. Conversation is the lifeblood of academic life, whether it is a conversation a scholar is having in the still silence of their research or through literary interaction with others in print or in face-to-face meetings. The blood of the theological academy has changed thanks to the presence of minorities, but this new blood does not yet circulate with ease through the body. Racial and ethnic voices emerged as an interruption within the scholarly conversations of the theological academy and initially they made visible one dynamic that had always been present in the wider academy and society in America—the dynamic of intellectual assimilation and scholarly mimicry. That dynamic may be put crudely with a question: was the nonwhite scholar to be seen as (for example) a New Testament scholar who just happens to be black or brown and/or female or was their scholarship marked by and defined through their race and gender?

This dynamic, which pivoted on the idea of authentic/inauthentic identities, had the unintended consequence of making visible the racial subject in theological work (that is, the identity of the scholar and not just their scholarship) and brought white identity into view, no longer concealed inside of claims to objectivity or universality. This dynamic blossomed into a wider set of issues that now highlight the troubled status of academic theological conversation. Racial and ethnic minorities have witnessed the fragmentation of conversation. That fragmentation is not due primarily to the explosion of knowledge, or the increased specialization within the theological disciplines, or the increased number of scholars entering the fields. That fragmentation is due to the disjointed lines of interlocutors now at play in the theological academy. Who is talking to whom? Who is listening? Under what conditions are people speaking? These have become very complicated questions in scholarly work and scholars of color are caught in very serious negotiation regarding the lines of communication. On one side you have scholars who are trying to think the constitutive realities of their subject matter in relation to the constitutive realities of identities and of contemporary social structures and on the other side you have scholars who resist such a concurrence, preferring to imagine their subject matter enclosed within its own internal logics and order of knowing that are only compromised by identity matters. Indeed, quite a few scholars on this latter side imagine a continuing decline in their scholarly fields because of such wrongheaded subjective inquiry. Both groups of scholars are concerned with the advancement and clarification of knowledge in their fields, but the kind of conversation necessary for the furtherance of knowledge is not clear to everyone. Even at this moment, there remains a racial/ethnic/gender divide in the conversations of the theological academy with people of color and their allies in one discursive orbit and significant numbers of white scholars in another discursive orbit. Each recognizes the existence of the other, sometimes in polite scholarly acknowledgment but rarely in shared intellectual exploration. The question now is whether there will emerge a generation of scholars that can embody new forms of interaction and intellectual exchange that mark a new reality of shared conversation and projects that enhances knowledge.

Living in Someone Else's House

Teachers of color entering the theological academy entered curricular houses and institutional ecologies not built with them in mind, often asking the abiding question: when and where do I enter? The usefulness of the house or all its aesthetic pleasures was not in question. The real question was the status of the new occupants. The presenting question in regard to institutional ecologies and curricular structures was and is the cost of adaptation. What does it cost the scholar of color and what does it cost the institution to adapt to this new life together? Making an old house fit new occupants is exhausting work with mixed results. Such has been the case with minority scholars in predominately white institutions. One of the untold stories of theological education in the last sixty years has been the painful struggle of scholars of color to thrive in these institutions. There is a trail of tears of minority faculty members that match a trail of missteps and backwards steps by institutions. At issue has been the willingness of institutions to receive fully the changes that minority faculty members bring to the articulation of their disciplines, to the teaching of their subject matter, and to administrative leadership. What comes along with those changes is the rearticulation of the mission of the school. What has also been at issue is the willingness of racial and ethnic minority faculty members to take on the missional trajectories of the institution in ways that announce deep continuity with its most cherished hopes.

What complicates further this new life together is the powerful inertia embedded in predominately white theological institutions toward recapitulating a centered white male subject as the abiding image of education being done well. Racial and ethnic faculty (and students) struggle against the phantasm of the white male in the classroom. That haunting presence of an authorial norm often invades faculty-student interactions and the way minority faculty members are positioned in relation to their discipline and their teaching. Many are pressed toward shadow boxing with an image they cannot defeat. Worse yet, faculty members in general are tempted toward a kind of phantom assimilation, a spirit possession through which they mimic the comportment and gestures of a mythical white male subject in both the way they articulate their discipline and their teaching. In truth, theological institutions count on a reality of assimilation in order to sustain their theological and pedagogical traditions. However, that assimilation, when embedded in the historical trajectories of white male subject formation, works against the healthy cultivation of a faculty and tempts some toward racial and gender mimicry.

What constitutes a discipline being presented well and teaching being done well is an open question in the theological academy. That question has now emerged with a new intensity in institutions with an increased presence of nonwhite faculty. This new intensity is due in great measure to the crumbling assumptions regarding both *who* guarantees excellent teaching (a white male teacher) and *what* guarantees high quality theological education. That latter guarantee was rooted in the imperial position that theological instruction enjoyed in Western educational systems. Gone is the day when theological studies (broadly understood) enjoyed its foundational status in the formation of a cultivated individual. Theological studies was woven into liberal arts education in such a way as to make its pedagogical justifications invisible and made it unnecessary to articulate its goals in formation. But the form of excellence in scholarship and teaching and student cultivation is now precisely what demands clarification through a new conversation. However, not many theological faculties have found their way toward sustaining a productive conversation regarding the form of excellence in theological education. That conversation has not gained significant traction because faculties have been slow to articulate to themselves the lines of continuity and discontinuity of disciplinary and pedagogical vision that are implicit and sometimes explicit with a diverse faculty.

Racial and ethnic faculty members often find themselves in an interrupted status. The real conversation about who they are and what their work means for the very nature of the school's educational endeavor is not happening. The real conversation about the difference their scholarship and presence make to the ecology of the classroom is not happening. The necessary conversation about serious reform to the curricular vision of the school because of their intellectual presence will not happen. And the important conversation about how the faculty together must carry forward the missional aspirations of the institution as new wine in new wineskins is also not happening. A perennial symptom of this interrupted status is the continuing practice of placing the teaching work of racial and ethnic faculty members in ancillary roles in relation to the core pedagogical thrust of the curriculum. That ghettoized positioning shows poor institutional self-reflexivity in its thinking about how it transitions from its past to its future. It also marks the ambiguity that continues to cover minority presence in many institutions where it has not been made clear that their intellectual work and presence is a welcomed and celebrated good thing.

The issue here is related but different from the resistance that many scholars of color experienced as the first generation of minority scholar at their institutions. The issue here has to do with their presence in relation to how the institution thinks of itself and understands its work in society and the world. In this regard, the intellectual presence of racial and ethnic faculty members has not penetrated to the core of institutional reflection on good scholarship, teaching, and student formation. The question now in this regard is what real difference does racial and ethnic (and gender) difference make for how theological institutions do their reflective work, especially with a view toward student formation?

Forming Students in Which Century?

Many predominately white theological institutions have now had several generations of students of color move through their halls. Indeed most of the racial and ethnic faculty members of today were the minority students taught in many cases by those first-generation minority faculty members. Together they share a powerful legacy of successful adaptation to their institutions in ways that allowed them to make productive use of their theological training. Adaptation however has not thus far meant the kind of transformation of institutional ethos that would create a deep collaboration of formation goals for diverse students. The weight that borders on being a burden of figuring out how to adapt the theological formation that takes place in the institution to preparing them to face the real needs of racial and ethnic communities remains on the shoulders of students. This burden is beyond the usual challenge of translating the world of theological discourse within common everyday language and merging the knowledge formed in the academy with the good wisdom of indigenous communities. This burden draws students of color into the exhausting task of trying to map the complexities of life in the racial world across the complexities of theological formation without enough help.

That exhausting task is made even more problematic by its fragmentation within the theological academy, which aligns minority students with their own private labors, African American, Hispanic, Asian, African and so forth—each invited to figure out the relevance of their theological formation for their own communities. Very few theological institutions have at this moment developed a strategic vision of deep collaboration that pulls the burden off the bodies of minority students and returns it to the shared work of the entire community. That work of helping minority students in this regard tends to fall heavily on racial and ethnic minority faculty members who are yet pulled into the relentless work of trying to establish the conditions for relevance. What are the conceptual conditions necessary for the work of the theological academy to be relevant to the communities that draw my concern? What are the conditions necessary for my scholarly work to be relevant to the concerns of my communities? The value of such questions is not at issue, only their reach. These should be the questions of the entire theological community, but they tend to be isolated to the faculty and students of color. That isolation penetrates many institutions, leaving untapped the potential to bring various minority students along with white students into a shared project of collaborative formation that might bring their communities together.

Ironically, this lack of collaborative formation continues to stunt the growth of white students, many of whom recognize that they must be able to function within the new multicultural realities of society and who don't want to embody and perform a preferred homogeneity through their ministries and by their lives. Developing a vision of collaborative formation requires institutions to reflect on the foundational image(s) that drives their work of formation. Many institutions that are beginning to challenge the idea of a center/margin in the classroom have not begun to challenge that conceptual arrangement in the formation process of students. Many schools opt out of such work, preferring to leave to minority faculty members and students the strange work of creating a parallel universe of formation—of spiritual, ministerial, and intellectual formation that runs alongside the central work of the institution. The question now is whether theological schools can more deeply collaborate with racial and ethnic students concerning their formation needs and if they can envisage formation that cross-pollinates and interpenetrates spiritual visions so that all students are invited into a truly shared project of cultivation that is not assimilation into a white norm. The hope in this regard would be to cultivate in students an ability to foster such collaboration in and between faith communities.

Conclusion

What a prospective student of color will see if she visits a theological school today would be markedly different and better than what she would have seen five or six decades ago. Yet what she would see is a very serious work in progress. Theological institutions in North America (and the Western world) are still moving beyond their colonialist groundings. They are however yet to shake free from their segregationalist habits of mind. The question remains whether they can and will start to imagine with the multitude, that is, imagine a diverse church and diverse communities not to manage but to embody through their educational processes and their common life. Theological education in the Western world has entered a new stage where it must develop authentically decolonial habits of mind that transform theological schools into places that educate people toward one another and not simply beside one another.

8

Why Seminaries and Churches Should Welcome Religious Diversity in the USA

Heidi Hadsell

Now, almost two decades into the twenty-first century, it is possible to discern the impact that growing religious diversity in the United States has begun to have on at least some institutions of theological education and the people and the churches they serve.

The habitat of post-World War II mainline and evangelical Christian seminaries was primarily in the expanding American middle class. In recent decades this once expanding population and economic base of what was the hegemonic religion in the United States has been contracting, resulting in churches closing, funds diminishing, aggregating and ecumenical organizations like the National Council of Churches shrinking or disappearing, and fewer seminary students enrolling in fewer seminaries. An article in the book *White Christian America is Dying*, written by Robert Jones, succinctly describes the massive generational shift going on in American Christianity:

> Today, young adults ages 19 to 29 are less than half as likely to be white Christians as seniors 65 and older. Nearly 7 in 10 American seniors (67 percent) are white

Christians, compared to fewer that 3 in 10 (29 percent) young adults."[1]

Over the decades of the contraction of mainline Christianity, there has been, coincidentally, a slow but steady increase in religious pluralism in the USA. This is due primarily to the Immigration and Nationality Act of 1965, which, by abolishing the quota system based on national origins, opened the doors to immigrants from all over the world who, naturally, brought their religions with them to the USA. These religious communities are slowly finding their voices in civic communities, developing relationships with their Christian and Jewish interlocutors in churches and synagogues and other religious institutions, and taking steps towards institutionalizing their religious traditions in this new context. Today, according to the Pew Foundation, religious diversity has increased so much in the United States that one in five adults have grown up in a family of more than one religion.[2]

The changing religious demographics over time have become visible to many and they raise implicit and explicit moral and theological questions to churches and the seminaries and denominations that serve them, about Christian relationships with people of other faiths, beginning with the age old question of "who is my neighbor?"

Theological educators are responding and will continue to respond to the questions posed by the religious diversity found right here at home, in a wide variety of ways. These responses will be shaped by many factors including denominational identities, histories, and theologies, predominant theological orientations, readings of civic responsibility, geographical locations, relations with and experiences with local communities of people of other faiths, faculty voices and interests, and student demand.

The pace of change in approaches to, and awareness of, the importance of the theme of interfaith education in seminaries

1. Jones, Robert, "White Christian America is Dying," *The Washington Post*, August 15, 2016.

2. Lipka, Michael, "Few Americans identify with more than one religion," http://www.pewresearch.org/fact-tank, (October 26, 2016)

over the last twenty years has been relatively rapid. In the late 1990s, Hartford Seminary's Muslim Chaplaincy Program was new, the appropriateness and adequacy of the words *chaplain* and *chaplaincy* was still being debated in Muslim communities, and, for the most part, Christian theological seminaries were places where Christians studied, not Muslims or other people of other faiths. Hartford Seminary, having studied Islam seriously for well over a hundred years, and with Muslims on the faculty, was fairly unique in Protestant theological education, and its unique profile made Hartford Seminary an ideal place for a Muslim chaplaincy program.

That was more than two decades ago. Today, the Muslim chaplaincy program at Hartford Seminary continues to thrive. Across the USA, there are other Muslim chaplaincy programs in several Protestant seminaries, and educational institutions established, financed, and run by Muslims are also appearing with increasing strength and speed. Some seminaries are hiring full-time faculty or adjuncts to teach Judaism, Hinduism, Islam, or Buddhism to seminary students, and increasing numbers of faculty in increasing numbers of disciplines have begun to address interfaith issues and dynamics as core elements in their disciplines. Cooperation between Christian seminaries and institutions or communities of people of other faiths have vastly multiplied, and there is a lively conversation among and between seminaries who see interfaith education, variously defined, as a growing part of their vocation.

This conversation and the growth of various forms of and approaches to interfaith education in a number of seminaries is sufficiently robust that it seems safe to say that over the next decade or more, unless something dramatic intervenes, there will be considerable helpful and creative experimentation, and the pursuit of different models of just how best to engage, and how thoroughly to engage in interfaith teaching and learning. The models will change as Christian communities change, as the society changes, but also and importantly, as the other religious communities in the United States change, and as they further institutionalize on American soil.

Churches Should Welcome Religious Diversity

Already, as indicated above, a variety of emerging models, or perhaps more accurately, experiments with models of interfaith theological education have appeared over the last two decades. They range from somewhat tentative academic nods to the growing interest in and interfaith nature of the US society, to more full-blown and elaborate interfaith educational programs, involving different faith communities in conversation and cooperation in new educational endeavors. Thus, for example, some seminaries offer courses in Islam, Judaism, or Hinduism or another religion or religions, providing the opportunity for their students to learn the basics about another tradition. Some seminaries use Christian faculty to teach such courses and some prefer to hire faculty, often adjuncts, from the tradition about which they are teaching.

Several seminaries see themselves as more or less temporary partners with people from another tradition who wish eventually to start their own seminary in their own patterns, but who for the present time need institutional space, perhaps some educational and accrediting know-how, and more financial resources in order to do so. This model, which involves Christian seminaries enrolling students from non-Christian traditions, for programs that are seen as transitory in the long run, is one that some call "incubating" theological education for another tradition.

Another approach is for seminaries to seek cooperation with Jewish seminaries or Muslim or other religious communities in response to the fresh interest of their own students in getting to know people from other religious communities. In this way, even as a seminary remains fully Christian, its cooperation on programs or activities of various kinds with a seminary or another organization of another religion, provides opportunities for students to encounter and engage students of other traditions in significant ways.

There are also many examples of practical cooperation between for example, Christian and Jewish seminaries, on things like CPE programs, that were perhaps initially motivated primarily by practical convenience and economic necessity, but that then became important sites for interfaith interaction and cooperation.

Also, there are rapidly growing numbers of opportunities for seminary students and others to engage with others across faith traditions in special programs of travel and study.

A number of seminaries have devised separate educational paths through degree programs for students of different faiths. These seminaries are in important ways interfaith, and the students have ample opportunity to interact, but the academic paths they pursue through the institution are essentially parallel.

At Hartford Seminary, the model that has emerged over many years is integrated education. By this I mean that even those programs intended for specific professional preparation, such as Muslim chaplaincy, provide opportunity, and in fact, require that the students take courses not just in their own tradition, but in another tradition. Students thus regularly encounter other religious traditions academically and engage with students and faculty from other religious traditions in the classroom. When I teach Christian Ethics I expect to have Muslim students and/or Jewish students in the classroom.

Helping to prepare the ground for such personal and academic encounter that many students have had little experience with before they enter Hartford Seminary, is a required course for all MA students entitled "Dialogue in a World of Difference," taught by a team of Jewish, Muslim, and Christian faculty members. Interestingly, although the faculty did not foresee this, over time the Doctor of Ministry program has emerged as one of the popular programs for interfaith engagement and education. It turns out that leaders of different religious communities find they have much in common as they think about the dynamics of their communities and the challenges of leadership in their communities. Also, the DMin program is a welcome opportunity for many pastors, imams, and rabbis to get to know in significant ways not just leaders of one's own religious community but leaders of other religious communities as well.

As mentioned above, coincidentally, as communities of people from religions beyond Christianity and Judaism have grown over the last several decades in the USA, communities of

Churches Should Welcome Religious Diversity

Christians in the USA have shrunk. Many seminaries are finding themselves with shrinking numbers of students, classrooms that aren't filled, housing that is partially empty, libraries that are being underused, and so forth. The presence of people of other faiths in their civic communities seems to some seminaries like an opportunity for recruitment that could result in increased enrollments, greater financial stability, and thus good stewardship of the physical and academic assets of the seminary.

It will be interesting to see how, over time, institutions that have embarked on an interfaith future more out of financial need and desire for good institutional stewardship, and less out of a deep vocational commitment, endure. Surely the experience itself can be so compelling as to be transformative for the institution in terms of motivation and perspective. However, interfaith education, which is complex, demanding, delicate, slow, often expensive, and full of questions and unexpected road blocks, would seem to be an educational endeavor only really worth the effort in the long run, for those schools for whom it is a genuine vocation.

Part of the vocation of theological education, at least theological education that is ecumenical, is predicated on the genuine appreciation for the integrity, depth, and wisdom of the traditions of the students who enroll. The assumption must be that we benefit from and learn from each other. This is the case in relation to the diversity of Christian students within ecumenical seminaries, and it must also be the case in relation to students from other religious traditions in institutions that once were exclusively Christian. Students who are not Christian must be able to fully trust that their faith, their religious tradition, is honored and respected within the institution in which they enroll. And the welcome extended to them by the institution must have no hidden agendas.

Seminaries that take interfaith education seriously and enroll students from other traditions and employ faculty from other traditions will find that they have many things to think about. First and foremost in my experience is their relationship with and responsibility not just to the students who enroll, but also to the faith communities from which the students and faculty come. These are communities who have in a real sense entrusted their students to the care of the seminary and they should be thought of and respected as partners with the seminary in the educational journey of their students.

Partnerships and friendships of one kind or another, the articulation of common goals and values, opportunities to learn informally as well as formally from each other, are critically important as essential building blocks as interfaith programs are launched or even just thought about. I cannot imagine the Hartford Seminary Muslim chaplaincy program or other Hartford Seminary programs related to relationships between Muslims and Christians and Jews, without the informal and formal partnerships and friendships of the seminary with Muslim and Jewish communities near and far .

These partnerships and friendships have been critical to the success of these programs, both in terms of all kinds of cooperation, support and academic contributions, but also and very importantly, ideas, feedback, and community connections and networks. Hartford Seminary's programs in Islam and Muslim Christian relations could never have flourished as they have without sustained, committed Muslim individuals and mosques, supportive of our work, trusting us with their students, and willing to be critical friends. Some of these friends are or have been on the board of trustees and have served the seminary formally in a number of other ways as well.

The relationships between Christian communities and other communities of faith in the United States already inevitably take place within the global context, and the awareness and weight of this global context will only increase. The global nature of our traditions, the scale and scope of human immigration, the speed and ease with which humans can communicate to even remote corners of the world, promise a world that will be ever more globally intertwined and interconnected.

Contemporary relationships across faith traditions are inevitably colored by, shaped by, informed by relationships and histories that are often many hundreds of years old and from various corners of the world. Christianity is growing most rapidly in the southern hemisphere and as it grows the importance of the nature of the relationship between Christians and people of other faiths in the southern hemisphere grows also.

It is thus not surprising that the students who first alerted me to the urgency of the question of the relationship of Christians to peoples of other faiths were students from countries outside the United States, mostly parts of Asia and Africa. At that time I was the Director of the Ecumenical Institute of the World Council of Churches, whose educational task it is to foster in young leaders from around the world, ecumenical understanding at the graduate level, and academic knowledge about other Christian traditions and the history of ecumenical relationships between traditions. Because many of the students came from contexts in which the interfaith relationships were at least as pressing and important as were the ecumenical relationships, and sometimes much more urgent, they raised questions in countless ways about how the Ecumenical Institute (Bossey) could help them think about interfaith relationships in addition to ecumenical relationships and histories. The students had very vivid experiences that sent them in search of answers, practical tools, theologies, ethics, histories that would help them figure out how to best engage people of other faiths and also how to talk about, preach about, and think about people of other faiths.

Eventually, after talking and thinking with colleagues at Bossey and also working with and learning from colleagues in the office of interfaith relations at the WCC, we dedicated a graduate semester to this theme of dialogue with other religions. The semester included trips of the Bossey students to visit religious leaders—Jewish, Muslim, Hindu, Buddhist—at their places of worship in and around Geneva. The eagerness of the Bossey students—themselves young leaders of Christian communities around the world—for this opportunity to literally cross the threshold and enter the worship space of another tradition, and engage people of that tradition in conversation, coupled with the very real fear some of them expressed as they did so, brought home to me just how pressing this moral and theological theme was for these students and for the congregations and denominations they served. Several years later, having accepted the position as President of Hartford Seminary, a school with many decades of interfaith experience, especially between Muslims and Christians, I remember staring out the window of a plane, thinking about how to help American Christians understand the importance of our relationships with people of other faiths, a theme, which is, while it might not have seemed so then in the spring of 2001, central to the identity and moral responsibility of North American Christians every bit as much as it is to Nigerians or Indonesians.

Of course, the question of relations with people of other faiths is one that has been the topic of debate and discussion since the earliest of Christian communities. Hartford Seminary itself had debated this question off and on for 150 years. The seminary acquired its expertise in Islam and Muslim Christian Relations in the final decades of the nineteenth century and the first few decades of the twentieth century, when it served as a primary educational center for Protestants going into the mission field, especially in Muslim majority countries. But by the end of the 1950s the seminary had rethought its relationship with Muslims and Islam and eventually decided to cease training missionaries who would use their knowledge of Islam, Muslim cultures, and Arabic to try to convert Muslims, and instead use the seminary's gathered wisdom and resources on Islam for a center of dialogue and study between Christians and Muslims.

In 1911 the faculty and board of Hartford Seminary revised the creed it had used since the establishment of the seminary in 1834, saying of the old creed "It was largely shaped by the controversies of its time. Moreover, it is the product of a controversial age in which differences were emphasized; whereas we are living in a generation that is seeking to minimize the doctrines which divide sincere Christians."[3] In so doing they reflected a spirit that persists at Hartford Seminary today as applied now not just to ecumenical relations but also to interfaith relations, as does their approach in

---

3. Geer, *The Hartford Theological Seminary*, 224.

Churches Should Welcome Religious Diversity

1911 which they described in this way: "The letter killeth but the Spirit giveth life." We believe we can best honor the fathers, not by following the letter of their creed and thus endangering in our lives the things which they hold most dear, but by re-expressing their spirit and following their method, doing for our time what they did for theirs through a creed that is as contemporary for us as theirs was for them. [4]

Ultimately interfaith education is a result of cooperation and trust between religious communities who are engaged in mutual and respectful relationships and dialogue and who become together a vehicle for helping students increase and sustain peaceful cooperation between peoples of different communities, even as they gain in their understanding and their knowledge of the specificities of their own faiths.

When the Islamic chaplaincy program began at Hartford Seminary more than two decades ago, no one could have imagined how successful the Hartford Seminary program and later other Muslim chaplaincy programs would be, and how popular the career of chaplaincy for Muslim men and women it helped give birth to would become. Today chaplaincy—Christian, Jewish, Muslim, Hindu—has emerged as a highly valued career for those who wish to serve their own communities here in the USA but want to do so in the midst of and in relationship to other communities.

The popularity of chaplaincy and other forms of ministry in interfaith settings is a good indication of the hunger many religious people have for engaging with others from other religions and also with others with no particular religion, who share similar values and dialogical goals. Theological education's task is to give people the scriptural, theological, and moral resources to deepen their own faith while they also learn about the religious faith of others and about the skills and the processes of dialogue and the construction of mutual relationships between them. Or as the tag line of Hartford Seminary puts it : "Exploring Differences, Deepening Faith." This is very much a task of the present and will be very much a task of the future we are helping to build today.

4. Geer, *The Hartford Theological Seminary*, 225.

Looking Forward with Hope

A small but growing number of Christian seminaries in the United States are already engaged in some form of interfaith theological education. This engagement seems likely to continue and even expand, although undoubtedly some of the attempts at interfaith educational engagement will not flourish or endure, for any number of reasons. What might be the result of the engagement in interfaith education in some seminaries over time?

From my perspective, having participated in eighteen years of such engagement at Hartford Seminary in the classroom and as president, the results have been and will continue to be quite positive educationally for Christians as well as for people of other faiths, and also positive in terms of benefits for the wider society. Here are some of the elements that go into this assessment and that have to do directly or indirectly with the increased numbers of people of other faiths in the USA and the corresponding increase in the awareness of religious diversity among American Christians.

- Knowledge about other religious traditions will increase in importance as part of the core curriculum of Christian theological education in the years ahead, as will relationships and partnerships with people and communities of other faiths.

- Awareness of and cooperation with friends and colleagues from other religious traditions will help Christians in general, including Christian leaders and Christian seminaries, feel newly enthusiastic about being Christian and newly aware of the specificity of just what it means to be Christian, so as to better converse with friends from other traditions.

- This awareness will help Christians see afresh, through the eyes of others, the value and the positive roles religions play in society. Working together with people from other religious traditions will help Christians get over their grief/bewilderment at their loss of hegemony in American society.

- Christians will learn how to better tell their own story and claim their own faith identity without disparaging those from other faiths, and this will free them for pursuing respectful and mutual relationships with people of other faiths. The model will be bridge-building, not conversion.

- Seminaries will help nurture a renaissance of Christian theological and ethical and pastoral thought about Christian life and belief and faithfulness in multi-faith contexts, and of exploration of what we might and should do together.

- There will continue to be an expansive growth in organizations that are multi-faith, some of which once were Christian or Christian and Jewish, as religious leaders discover the power and joy of working together across religious lines towards common goals and values. The whole society will benefit.

- Seminaries, in their awareness of who their students are and the religious and nonreligious nature of the American population, will be serious about and respectful of dialogue with and study of humanism/atheism, and will welcome students who are "spiritual but not religious" in their classrooms.

- The markers for or criteria of excellence and preparation of Christian leadership and ministry will include knowledge about other religious traditions and Christian relationships with them, and also knowledge about interfaith dynamics and interfaith families and other interfaith relationships.

- Christian seminaries will continue to pool and share resources with Jewish, Muslim, and other seminaries and educational institutions for things like CPE. Seminaries will find they need each other in order to fully prepare people for work within their traditions and will experiment with joint programs and various other forms of cooperation.

I will end with this: a prediction of sorts, and an observation that may serve as a calling for our seminaries. I suspect that in coming years there will be growth in careers such as chaplaincy (university, prison, hospital, armed forces) that require deep knowledge of and commitment to one's own religious tradition, and simultaneously, knowledge of and respect for other religious traditions and eagerness to work with, cooperate with, and learn from people from other religious traditions and their leaders.

Bibliography

Geer, C. M., *The Hartford Theological Seminary: 1834–1934*. Hartford, CT: The Case, Lockwood and Brainard, 1934.